What people are saying about *Living Happy to Be ME!*

"Valerie Sheppard's Living Happy to Be Me! *is a wonderful collection of compelling stories, powerful lessons and fun and practical exercises that will help you get on the path to living a truly happy life. This is a book to not only read but fully immerse yourself in."* ~ JACK CANFIELD, CO-AUTHOR OF THE CHICKEN SOUP FOR THE SOUL SERIES AND THE SUCCESS PRINCIPLES, FEATURED TEACHER IN THE SECRET

*"*Living Happy to Be ME! *is a great read. With wisdom and compassion, Valerie Sheppard helps us dismantle the false-self and awaken to the Divine presence in our heart...and she is a beautiful embodiment of what teaches."* ~ MARCI SHIMOFF, #1 NEW YORK TIMES BESTSELLING AUTHOR OF HAPPY FOR NO REASON, LOVE FOR NO REASON, AND CHICKEN SOUP FOR THE WOMAN'S SOUL

"Author Valerie Sheppard's unique teachings and artful imagery will tap into your soul regardless of the path you're currently walking, expanding your ability to be exquisitely happy. I highly recommend Living Happy To Be Me.*"* ~ DR. SHAWNE DUPERON, 6-TIME EMMY® WINNER, PROJECT: FORGIVE FOUNDER, 2016 NOBEL PEACE PRIZE NOMINEE

"In Living Happy to Be ME!*, Valerie Sheppard, one of the most original inspirers today, shows you how to unleash your inherent power to truly live exactly how your life was always intended to be—happy and deeply fulfilling."* ~ MARSH ENGLE, BESTSELLING AUTHOR, COACH AND SPEAKER

"This is simply the most beautiful book I've ever read. Surrender to this simple and profound process. You will want to keep it by your bedside and make it a part of your daily joy." ~ TERESA DE GROSBOIS, #1 INTERNATIONAL BESTSELLING AUTHOR OF MASS INFLUENCE, SPEAKER AND FOUNDER OF THE EVOLUTIONARY BUSINESS COUNCIL

"In Living Happy to Be ME!*, Valerie shares timeless wisdom and practical guidance. Her 4-Step process helps us get clear on who we really are so we can overcome anything in the way of our true happiness."* ~ JANET ATTWOOD, NEW YORK TIMES BESTSELLING AUTHOR OF THE PASSION TEST AND YOUR HIDDEN RICHES

"As a guide for going within to find and heal yourSelf, Living Happy To Be ME! is as good as it gets. Valerie Sheppard teaches as well as touches our hearts and minds with references to the works of everyone from Monty Python to the Dalai Lama. If you're looking for a reliable map to what's going on inside of you and how to lift yourself up and out of life's struggles and challenges, this is it!" ~ TONY BURROUGHS, CO-FOUNDER OF THE INTENDERS OF THE HIGHEST GOOD AND AUTHOR OF 10 BOOKS INCLUDING THE CODE: 10 INTENTIONS FOR A BETTER WORLD

"Living Happy to Be ME! is a beautiful, engaging book for cultivating life-time happiness. Sheppard's 4-Step process is insightful and effective. Get ready to experience a wonderful process of heart-opening and happiness building." ~ ELLEN ROGIN, CO-AUTHOR OF THE NEW YORK TIMES BESTSELLER PICTURE YOUR PROSPERITY

"Valerie's beautiful new book contains the ingredients for elevating our Consciousness to create more happiness, fulfillment, and success. She takes us on a transformational journey to greater, authentic happiness by sharing her personal stories, easy practical tools, and helping us build a foundation for a happy and vibrant life. This book has consciousness-raising tips and wisdom that can change the lives of millions. Be sure you're one of them!" ~ DAVID DACHINGER, CO-CREATOR OF LOVING MEDITATIONS

"A must-read! This book gives you a perspective-changing approach to experiencing profound happiness and a deeper connection with yourself. Insightful, and filled with powerful consciousness-raising activities." ~ MARILYN SUTTLE, BESTSELLING AUTHOR, WHO'S YOUR GLADYS?

"Simply brilliant! A must read for anyone who wants to turn their frown upside down." ~ GREG S. REID, CO-AUTHOR, THINK AND GROW RICH: THREE FEET FROM GOLD

"When applying the Law of Attraction the 'secret sauce' is attaching an elevated emotion to the movie you play in your head of this new outcome. Valerie has created the perfect practical guide in this book that will help you overcome emotional distress and other vibration-lowering obstacles so you can maintain the high emotions you need to attract your heart's desires." ~ NATALIE LEDWELL, BESTSELLING AUTHOR, TV HOST, SPEAKER AND CO-FOUNDER OF MINDMOVIES.COM

Living
Happy
To Be ME!

Living Happy To Be ME!

Dancing Your Soul Lightstyle

Valerie René Sheppard

The Heart of Living Vibrantly
San Clemente, CA

ISBN-13: 978-0-9963559-5-7

Library of Congress Control Number: 2016900708

Living Happy to Be ME! is published by:
The Heart of Living Vibrantly
San Clemente, CA

For information please direct emails to:
info@HeartofLivingVibrantly.com or visit our website:
HeartofLivingVibrantly.com

Book cover and interior design: Teri Rider

First Edition, June 2016

Printed in the United States of America

23 22 21 20 19 18 17 16   1 2 3 4 5 6 7 8 9

"It takes courage to be happy."
~Florence Henderson, Actress, Author, Singer

This book is dedicated to you, the reader,
and all the other courageous people who are willing to
take an inward journey of discovery and transformation to
raise their Consciousness.

Elevating your Consciousness is the only True way I know of to
create deep and lasting happiness in your life.

As each one of us takes personal responsibility
for claiming and living as our Divine Selves,
we heal ourselves from the illusion of separation
and together, we will heal the planet,
and create more Peace, Love, Joy and Freedom for all.

And so it is!

Contents

Contents

Acknowledgements

I am grateful to the many people and situations that have contributed to the writing of this book. It is the culmination of a many-faceted journey, filled with experiences and connections that continue to contribute to my awakening and spiraling upwards. My feelings of True Happiness are ever-expanding.

Thank you to...

The late Naia OneHeart Levitt and Lauren Card for your ideas and inspiration at the very beginning, when the book was simply going to be a "free report."

My editors, who contributed insight and wisdom to the shaping of this book.

My extended spiritual family, including my Unity of Tustin sisters and brothers, my Sacred Lollipop Ship Sisters, and my Sisters Light, I am deeply grateful. So many of you have been mentors, and I am thankful for your wisdom, candor and steadfast support of my gifts and message. You have held sacred space for my intention, especially when I had trouble seeing my way and claiming my wisdom.

My spiritual counselor Michael, thank you for helping me walk into the dark places, put down the burdens, and retrieve the lost fragments of the True ME. Your love and guidance continue to illuminate my path into wholeness and full expression of my Divine Soul-Being Self.

My Mom, international award-winning nature photographer Elwye Ess, thanks for helping me uncover and connect the many missing dots from my childhood, and for all that you have sacrificed along the way to give me every possible opportunity for success and happiness. Thanks too for your support and encouragement along the road to my renaissance.

All those who continue to stand by, support, nurture, and enjoy my path alongside me, I am loving the life I am creating, and I'm loving that you are a part of the journey. May this book and what I stand for in its creation and dissemination be ongoing sources of Divine Light and Love in your lives!

Valerie

Foreword

The first time I saw Valerie Sheppard, she was sitting across from me in a hotel conference room. It was September 2014, and we were both in Chicago to attend an annual meeting of the Evolutionary Business Council (EBC), a worldwide organization bringing leaders of vision together to expand global change. I noticed that she had this air of love and generosity and yes, happiness about her. When she offered her insights to the group, each was a unique and profound pearl of wisdom. Unfortunately, the interactive exercises had us "turn to the person sitting next to you." Since Valerie was across from me on the other side of the six foot round table, the exercises didn't give us a chance to speak directly. At lunch I ran out to another meeting and then had to leave the event early to catch the last flight out. Valerie and I never really connected.

I remember being on the plane that night and perusing my notes from the EBC meeting. When I came to the page where I'd written down one of Valerie's pearls, I felt a pang of disappointment that I hadn't gotten to know that brilliant, vibrant woman with the Cheshire Cat grin and the sparkling eyes. Somehow, I knew that as fellow leaders in the EBC, our paths would cross again soon!

But before that could happen, I received an e-mail with the subject: *Please send healing love to Valerie Sheppard.* The body of the e-mail read: *In case you have not yet heard, our wonderful friend and colleague Valerie Sheppard had a catastrophic stroke yesterday while facilitating a leadership workshop at the University of California, Irvine. She is in the ICU at HOAG Hospital in Newport Beach, California. Let's join together in sending her prayers, love, and healing energy.*

Her entire right side was paralyzed and she had lost her ability to speak. The prognosis was not good. We were all devastated. Yet the one comment I heard more often than any other was, "If anyone can defy the odds, it's Valerie."

And she did.

Just eight months later, at our 2016 annual EBC event, Valerie bravely mounted the steps to the stage to share her mesmerizing story of recovery and more pearls of wisdom on how to soar in your life, no matter what your circumstances. I turned to my friend Shawne with tears of awe streaming down my face and said, "She should write a book about her experience and what she did to stay so upbeat and happy."

Shawne lifted a stack of papers and pointed to a book underneath. It was the Advance Reading Copy of *Living Happy to Be ME!©*.

I eagerly grabbed it and found myself pulled into the rich, colorful world of happiness that Valerie had created inside the covers of this glorious book. I hesitate to even call it a book. *Living Happy to Be ME!* is more than that. It's a life-changing, profound, transformational *experience* that I guarantee will impact your life as it has mine.

There is a tremendous amount of pain and suffering on this planet we call home—and there are no quick fixes to alleviate it. People of all ages and walks of life are wandering around in the wilderness of their lives wanting to find their place of rest and rejuvenation, their space of wholeness and contentment. Some have hit their 'rock bottom;' others are desperately trying to stop their descent before it spirals out of control. It has always troubled me to know how many of them don't know what to do or where to turn for help.

Yet every once in a while someone like Valerie comes along and says, "I know what it's like to suffer. I know what it's like to grow up trying to grasp for happiness and having it be just out of reach. I know what it's like to think that fulfillment will come on the other side of your next achievement or degree or relationship or shiny object, only to be disappointed again and again and again. And yet I now know that true and lasting happiness is not only possible, whatever your life circumstance, I've created a roadmap to guide you there."

This roadmap is exquisite in its practicality and simplicity. You only need open-hearted desire and willingness to step into a new you and the new life you will create as you embody these principles. Make no mistake about this: your life wasn't meant to be hard; you weren't meant to struggle and prove. You were meant to dance and laugh and feel deeply satisfied with yourself and your life.

You are here to express the glorious nature of your Divine Self. And no matter where you stand right now—in a quagmire, on the edge of a cliff, lost in the forest, wandering in the desert, at a crossroads, or even close to the mountaintop but not close enough—the Essence of you is that: *Divine*. You are destined to have a higher and better experience, one that aligns with who you really, *really*, **really** are. But you must let go of what is not working for you on that quest, and take a different route.

If your desire is to free yourself from false and limiting beliefs, heal wounds from your past, and learn concrete ways to claim real and lasting inner peace and happiness, there really is no time like the present. *It's your turn to defy the odds.* It's your time to take life from marginal to magnificent. And, you don't have to continue on the road alone.

I personally invite you to join me and embark on what I know will be a fun and enlightening journey to that place called *Living Happy to Be ME!*. I think you will find as I have, that the beautiful teachings illuminated throughout the book will meet you wherever you are on your life's path and shepherd you home to the happiness and fulfillment awaiting within your own being.

Lots of people call themselves experts on love or success or happiness or relationships. Unfortunately, too many of them don't really walk their talk. Yet I believe we all have built-in authenticity meters and can sense incongruence a mile away. That's why it's so exciting to have the gift of this book: we can learn the secrets to living profoundly happy lives, and walk the path with a guide who has not only thoroughly researched and meticulously crafted a powerful message, but who is also congruent with it.

Thank you Valerie for creating this vehicle of transformation! I know that as each individual embodies its wisdom, they will experience a profound shift, and each will in turn contribute greater light to the world. I believe *Living Happy to Be ME!* will be a classic in the self-help space for years to come!

It's a true joy to call you my friend and an honor to endorse your work from the deepest place in my heart.

Debra Poneman, bestselling author, founder and CEO of Yes to Success Seminars, Inc., and co-founder of Your Year of Miracles, LLC.

Introduction

THE HISTORICAL PURSUIT OF HAPPINESS

Happiness is perhaps among the most studied states in the history of humankind. Perspectives on the source of happiness have been captured throughout the ages. Philosophers, psychologists, pop stars, think-tanks, and major universities like Stanford, MIT, Columbia, and Harvard, have pondered the nature of individual happiness and provided a host of suggested causal relationships and ways to be happier.

From Plato believing happiness had to do with wisdom and the pursuit of good character, to those who came after him who attributed it to money, pets, genetics, biochemistry and everything in between, you've probably heard, and perhaps pursued, more than one way to "be" happy.

As much as happiness has been studied to find its cause, happiness also has an effect. It has been shown to make people healthier and more productive and ultimately, more successful and fulfilled. Though many have postulated success and fulfillment as causes of happiness, in fact, happiness is the *precursor* to these states. The data backing this up has been mounting for years. Consider the following:

In a 1930 study of 180 Catholic nuns, researchers found a link to positive emotion and longevity. Using autobiographical sketches the nuns completed when they committed to a convent, the researchers correlated positive and negative life statements to how long the nuns lived. 90 percent of the nuns rated in the top quartile for happiness were alive at age 85; 70 percent of the ones in the lowest quartile of happiness were dead by age 85.

This shows how happiness over time builds up in our system and helps us. Similarly, 54 percent of the most cheerful quarter was alive at age ninety-four, as opposed to just 11 percent of the least cheerful quarter. Overall, the nuns whose autobiographies contained the most sentences expressing positive emotions lived an average of seven years longer than nuns whose stories contained the fewest.

Researchers suggest that if your goal is to live longer, you should make happiness a priority in every moment.

Several studies about the impact of positivity and happiness were referred to in a December 2010 edition of the magazine *The Economist*:

- John Weinman, professor of psychiatry at King's College London, monitored the stress levels of a group of volunteers and then inflicted small wounds on them. The wounds of the least stressed healed twice as fast as those of the most stressed.

- At Carnegie Mellon University in Pittsburgh, Sheldon Cohen infected people with cold and flu viruses. He found that happier types were less likely to catch the virus, and showed fewer symptoms of illness when they did.

- Professor Andrew Oswald and two colleagues, Eugenio Proto and Daniel Sgroi, cheered up a bunch of volunteers by showing them a funny film. Following the film, the subjects did mental tests and the results were compared to groups that had seen a neutral film, or no film at all. The ones who had seen the funny film performed +12 percent better.

A 2010 study from Columbia University examined whether good heart health is a result of feeling good (*Davidson, 2010*). They found that over a period of 10 years, increased positive mood was protective against the 10-year incidence of coronary heart disease.

A growing body of evidence from the Positive Psychology movement and elsewhere shows that positive employees outperform negative employees in terms of productivity, sales, energy levels, turnover rates and health care costs. According to Shawn Anchor, Harvard researcher and author of *The Happiness Advantage*, optimistic sales people outperform their pessimistic counterparts by up to 37 percent; and doctors with a positive mindset are 50 percent more accurate when making diagnoses than those who have a negative mindset.

The desire for happiness is universal! People from all walks of life on every continent desire more happiness and contentment in their lives. It is a great leveler of humanity. It seems that no matter how rich or poor, healthy or unhealthy, young or old, urban or rural, lonely or in relationships one is, there is a desire for more happiness. Simultaneously, there is debate and confusion as to how to get it. Importantly too, through all the scientific studies of happiness dating back to the 1950s, there's been no demonstrable shift over time. As a collective, we are not happier today in general than we were more than 60 years ago.

Since you've picked up this book, it's likely you're exploring your *own* connection to or disconnection from happiness. Perhaps you have become clear that there are areas of your life that aren't working for you. Perhaps things are okay, but you want *more* than okay. Whatever the reason, anytime you take stock of where you are relative to where you want to be, you win. It's the conscious choice to ask deep questions about yourself and seek the answers *within* that enable you to shift your life. This exploration can reveal the many gifts awaiting you when you do so. It is also the first step to finding your treasure—the beauty that can come into your life as you raise your Consciousness and take personal responsibility for being happy and fulfilled.

Your New True Path to Happiness!

You now stand at a crossroads of commitment. Will you forge a new and more fulfilling path for yourself, a choice to be **Living Happy To Be ME!**© Or will you stay in your status quo—your comfort zone instead? Trying something new in your life is like trying on new shoes: you have to walk around in them a little before you can really tell if they fit. And even when you get them home, you may need to "break them in." This is about embracing and embodying a new idea of who you are and taking a walk around as that new you to experience the fit. You will see how changing the way you do and experience things impacts your life. The goal is to adopt ways to move through a personal metamorphosis and enhance your experience of being fulfilled, successful, inspired, and **Living Happy To Be ME!**

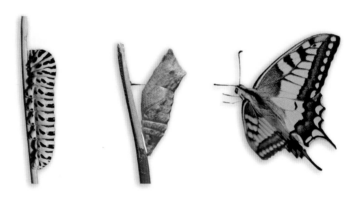

The Consciousness-raising **4 Step** process shared in this book is inspired by and tested in real life. Its application was central in my own personal transformation to a deeper place of authentic happiness, and it has also helped many others. Essentially, elevating your Consciousness is the only way I know of creating a life that is as successful as it is fulfilling. It's really how you reach your full potential, meaning you express your highest Divine Nature, and experience the rewarding world created from doing that.

Once you learn the **4 Step** process, this book also includes a host of ideas that are meant to be used "in the moment," as well as on a longer-term basis to help you to notice the state of your Consciousness, and then shift gears to raise it. Together, playing with all the tools I've provided enables a paradigm shift in the way you think about, define and express yourself. The more you explore the different options in different combinations, the higher the likelihood you will find things that are a perfect fit.

As you playfully and lovingly incorporate the foundational **4 Step** process, and then test your way through the other suggestions, things will naturally start to shift in the "You-ness" of you. There may be tears, laughter, fear, surprise, sadness and more as you uncover aspects of yourself that you may not have known existed. You will let go of things that may have been central to your old *idea* of yourself, and replace them with what is a more True fit.

You will likely find that many of your ideas are outdated and don't align with your inner wisdom. You may question how anything you are doing is what you *should* be doing. You will realize the many ways it has been *you* keeping yourself out of happiness and contentment, and not the people and situations in your outer world. You will begin to feel alive in ways you may not have thought possible. You will find the path of ease and Grace. You will feel yourself lightening up and letting go. You will feel an inner smile like never before!

All of this will be spectacular! It is your destiny as a Divine Being to know and fully express the Light of your True Nature. This book is designed to help you *remember* that nature, and that happiness is and always has been a part of it. *It is your inner state that dictates your outer experience.* When this idea goes from concept to belief within you, and from inner belief to embodied expression, you will experience your life shifting in magnificent ways.

Here is the ideal way to use this book. First, there is an overview of my

personal story. I want you to understand important pieces of the journey I've taken as a baseline. My intention is that you'll connect more deeply to where you are now in your life and how you can shift your position with these Steps. You may see yourself in aspects of me and my ways of being that help you get clarity and choose differently in your own life now. Know that it's never really about the story. It's about what the story can help you feel and understand that gets you closer to the Truth of who you are. So begin engagement with "Shedding the Masks."

Next, you'll find a section explaining the overall concept of **Living Happy To Be ME!** and the four powerful Steps that help you raise your Consciousness to get there. You **must** read this section before going into the rest of the book. There are several critical elements of how to make the Steps work in your life that are the heart and soul of aligning with your True Self. Until this foundation is established, the other aspects of the book can only take you so far. So please don't cheat yourself out of your own evolution by short-cutting.

The second half of the book is clustered into three sections addressing the different ways we generally engage in our lives: 1) through connection with Self, 2) through routines and habits, and 3) through connection with the world around us. Within each section, you'll find perspective that helps to set the stage, followed by a collection of suggestions for new ways to bring the more conscious You to full expression in your life.

I've structured these sections somewhat like a travel journal. There are lined pages for capturing thoughts, blank pages for doodles and drawings, inspirational quotes to provoke connection to your inner thoughts and feelings, and even places to paste photographs or other keepsakes along the way. I invite and encourage you to use them all!

As you will learn in the **Living Happy To Be ME!** instructional chapter, this is not a linear experience. Once you read through the tips and tools in the three later sections to familiarize yourself with what is there, you can do them randomly or in any order you choose. You should not start with the first one and work your way through them in the order they are presented. I would suggest you let your feelings guide you as to where to begin and what to do next. Connect internally with where you're feeling stuck. Is it your relationship to Self? Are you attached to your ways of doing things (routines)? Are you feeling disconnected from the world around you?

Let those feelings be the reason you start at a certain place, and trust that everything you choose to do after that will be contributing to your upward spiral.

Once you've chosen a section, choose a category and read the explanatory paragraph. Let it sink in. Then select a couple of the items to explore. You don't have to hurry; it's not a race. This journey takes as long as it takes. The important thing is that you do it.

Use the lined journaling pages to capture your thoughts, feelings, and any resolutions you make after each experience. What did you like and dislike? What new information about yourself did you discover? Write about how the activity made you feel emotionally before getting into the more intellectual aspects of it. For example, did you feel sadness, anger, or fear? What was the nature of any internal obstacles you had to overcome? Can you trace those obstacles to a particular experience from your childhood? What might you do differently in the future to make your experience more uplifting, enjoyable, and fun? What did you uncover about how you do life that can help you evolve your Consciousness so that you are more happy and fulfilled?

As you successfully overcome your obstacles and release your limitations, note how you did it, along with your new results. When did you feel yourself detaching from a limiting belief about yourself or about life? In what ways did you discover a deeper aspect of you? Don't think of it as "journaling" per se, but of a place to keep track of your successes and chart a course to the next stop on the journey. Use your writing to help take you deeper and further into the **4 Step** process. If you're using this book as part of one of my college course curriculums or coaching programs, your notes and reflections will contribute to what we do in private and group discussion sessions.

> *One way to be with past things that tends not to sap you of good feelings is to be in the role of a bystander or observer, and keep your judging self in neutral.*

Whatever you do, remember that this is supposed to be about elevating your Consciousness to create more happiness, fulfillment, and success. Even if there are difficult revelations or sorrowful memories, the journey shouldn't be debilitating and unpleasant. You don't have to relive the past by exploring it. One way that you can over-stay your time in the past is to get caught in judging, blaming, shaming and 'guilting' yourself about what you did or didn't do, and whether it was right, wrong, or your best. Focusing on the ideas of "right" and "wrong" in any situation can send you off track. Doing it about things you cannot change can make it impossible to get the wisdom from the experience and move on. One way to be with the past that tends *not* to sap you of good feelings is to be in the role of a bystander or observer, and keep your judging self in neutral. Try to look at whatever is coming up as though it's a story about someone you don't even know. As Eckhart Tolle offers in his book, *A New Earth*, it can help to say "is that so?" as you contemplate whatever you're reviewing. There's more on this concept of detachment later in the book. The important thing is to let go of as much judgment as possible, and keep going with the exploration.

Remember to laugh, be playful, and take yourself lightly! If you goof up at your dance classes, dislike the new veggie you bought, or get bitten by mosquitoes on your wilderness walk, let that be okay. This is a journey that's meant to be an adventure, an experiment, an opportunity to explore, awaken and discover more of the You-ness and True-ness of You. Go easy on yourself. By saying yes to this journey, you are calling in Divine support and love. Do your best to be open, and trust, allow, and receive the wisdom that comes to you.

I invite you now to turn the page and enter the realm of discovering the Divine Nature of you ... your own **Magnificent Essence!**

With blessings, love, and light!
Valerie

The Teachings

SHED YOUR MASKS

Personality, identity, beliefs, and story can be powerful influencers in our lives. In fact, they can be masks that cover up what we don't accept about ourselves—what we don't want others to see about us. Sometimes, putting the mask on is a totally conscious act, like when you put on a "happy face" in the midst of a difficult time. But a lot of the time, the masks are a part of a subconscious trigger designed to compensate for or protect us from some inner belief about the world and ourselves.

I now know that I spent a lot of time seeing my life from behind various masks as though they were the real me. I created them through the twists, turns, ups, and downs of my life, starting from when I was just a twinkle in my parents' eyes, and had breathed into them as the outward expression of what I thought was my inner "truth." I used them to help me feel accepted, powerful, capable, and to give me a place in the world.

I kept people at a distance or I pulled people closer through them. I felt secure relating through a work title or salary. I measured myself relative to others through my collection of stuff or my home address. I felt belonging through my personality traits or my credentials. I felt worthiness and confidence from my accomplishments and success. I could see where I fit, *and* where I didn't. Or so I *thought*. Identity, personality, beliefs, and the mental stories we tell ourselves are like a favorite old sweatshirt that always makes us feel good…and safe.

Interestingly, just like that beloved sweatshirt, these created pieces of ourselves can only go so far to hide what's underneath. Under the surface, I wasn't really feeling the confidence, strength, security, and worthiness that my outward actions would suggest. What was hidden from the world, and ultimately what *I* was hiding from, were deep-seated ideas of myself as being "less than." I had experienced early in my life, feeling like I was not good enough, smart enough, talented enough, capable enough, or lovable enough to be accepted by the world, or to ultimately be fulfilled and happy. I knew something wasn't right, but I *thought* it was with the world around me. I had no idea the trouble was within.

Some of the subconscious "trouble" was related to my experiences growing up in two different and powerfully influential cultures. First, I was a Black child born in the beginning of the 1960's. My parents were God-fearing, hard-working, good-hearted people from inner-city Baltimore. Born in the 1930's, they'd lived through the dynamic and sometimes most horrific and frightening aspects of the White vs. Black racial divide in the United States. This was the era of "Separate-but-Equal," racial terrorism in the form of the atrocities of the Ku Klux Klan, lynchings, bombings, riots, and assassination.

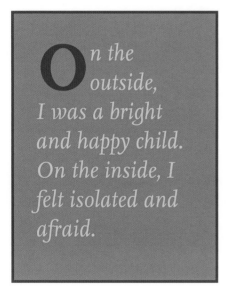

On the outside, I was a bright and happy child. On the inside, I felt isolated and afraid.

There were places Black people didn't dare go in the U.S. (or stay after the sun went down) if they wanted to get home alive. Black men could be tarred and feathered for simply looking at a White woman. I often heard the adults saying things like, "Black people have to work twice as hard to get half as much." From the things I heard and saw around me, I picked up how difficult and dangerous it was for people who were born Black in this country.

My baby book has my mother's hand-written story of my parents' pilgrimage to the Capitol to see assassinated President John F. Kennedy lying in state. Around me were the energies and emotions of fear, sadness, anger, and resentment, at the experiences of being here. It could at any moment mean you would pay the ultimate price for possibly the tiniest of offenses. While there was still immense and deep pride in the race, I picked up on mental and emotional levels how difficult it had been, and how potentially out of control life could be for people who looked like me. My early years were full of discipline, manners, and responsibility, as my parents taught me how to measure up in the predominantly White culture in ways I *could* control.

The second culture in our household was that of a disciplined, high-expectations, career Marine father. SEMPER FI! And he wasn't just any Marine. He was a Mustang—one who had enlisted at age 17, and instead of going to Officer Candidate School to become an officer, he worked his way up through the enlisted ranks and was eventually *promoted* to officer. In other words, he got to Captain the *hard* way—striving and struggling up the mountain. There were many rules in our house that dictated my behavior. I didn't dare talk back, I answered everything with "sir" and "ma'am," and it was pretty much *his* way or the highway. In fact, *his* way to wake us up in the morning was to burst into the room, turn on the light and shout "REVELIE!" *His* way often involved a belt.

On the outside, I was a bright and happy child. On the inside, I felt isolated and afraid. I didn't think my civilian friends could relate to the military experiences I was having. I also felt like people held preconceived notions about me and what I was capable of because I was Black. With the exception of the neighborhoods around my grandparents' homes in Baltimore, my brother and I were often among only a few Black children in all of our environments, including the many elementary schools and extra-curricular activities we explored through life as "Marine brats."

I was convinced I would forever be measured *first* by the color of my skin. At an early age, these feelings inside me began to show up in the outer expression of myself. Personality traits were born.

I declared, "Let Balerie do it!" as a toddler—the first statement of the "independent

and strong" *I* labeled myself as a girl, and *others* labeled me as a woman later in life. Living on military bases and the many moves we made as a Marine Corps family exacerbated the separateness I already felt. I experienced an almost constant undercurrent of fear: fear of being excluded, not being liked, of being alone, and of leaving right when I'd finally made a good friend. I learned to fear showing weakness, so I lived in a prison—of my own creation—being afraid to feel or talk about fear.

As children do, I created beliefs and behaviors to cope with my interpretations of who I was and how I was experiencing my life. If I was going to stand out, it would be for things that would help me feel secure and loved. I learned to work hard, take charge, and *excel*, so there'd be plenty of positive things to measure to compensate for what I thought others were thinking about me because of the color of my skin. I became competitive, aggressive, and driven, as I focused on powerfully telling the world who I was and what I was capable of despite being Black.

I had friends with whom I shared laughter and adventures. I was a Brownie and a Girl Scout. I participated in extracurricular activities like dance, sailing, and swim team. I made Honor Rolls, won track and field titles and soccer trophies. I was named Captain of this, Director of that, and was labeled *smart cookie, talented athlete,* and *born leader*. Yet, inside, I often felt like I didn't fit in, didn't count, like they didn't really *see* me, and like I was never enough.

I told myself their lives were better and mine didn't measure up. They liked their other friends better than me, and I wasn't really invited to the good stuff. The accomplishments and successes were fulfilling for short periods of time, but the feelings of pleasure they gave me never lasted very long. The moments of pride in myself were short-lived, and it was quickly back to the next proving ground. Were all these ideas true? Even if they weren't in actuality, they were my perception— they were the stories I told myself.

The older I grew and the more exceptional, accepted and liked I tried to become, the less I really felt those things were what I really was. Instead, I often felt like I was a misfit for one reason or another wherever I went. In high school, I was called "Oreo," by some of the other Black kids for "being Black on the outside but acting White on the inside." It wasn't unusual to be the only Black girl in most environments, and I was sure the White kids looked at me differently too. No matter how good I was at speaking or doing things, my dark skin made it obvious I couldn't be "one of them." So I actually didn't feel welcome with my Black or White peers. I didn't get into the popular sorority and I didn't win my race for class president.

I was once told that I was actually a "*double* negative" because I was not just Black, I was also female. Regardless of the accolades and recognition I received, I never believed inside that *my* A's, bright ideas, disciplined behavior, and top-notch abilities were treated with the same respect and adoration given to others around me. It was as if the world was telling me that I was not very welcome. At least that was my *interpretation* of what was going on.

Throughout it all, I did my best to ignore the sadness, fear, and resentment I was feeling, giving it little if any outward energy or expression. I generally sucked it up, stuffed it down and kept striving. I wasn't fully *pretending* to be happy, but I was definitely wearing a "making-the-best-of-it" happy mask. I figured if I resisted the thoughts and memories that didn't feel good, they would just go away. As long as I kept trying to prove my worthiness, I would eventually be delivered to my promised land.

I found a copy of Norman Vincent Peale's *The Power of Positive Thinking* on my grandmother's book shelf and read it when I was 13. Shortly thereafter, Grammy gave me a subscription to The *Daily Word*. I read it every day. It helped a lot. I loved the peacefulness I felt as I spent time with the passages and quotes, and interestingly, today, I love using powerful quotes as part of inspiring and teaching others. I practiced positive thinking and did my best to stay hopeful. But even with the positive support the readings provided, they were not really changing me at the core

> **I was conditioned to suffer through, to grin and bear it, to buck up and get it done.**

level. I didn't know it then, but as I look back, I was hiding from the negative emotions piling up under the surface by focusing elsewhere. I thought it was a way of "rising above" my circumstances, but it wasn't really working.

The Valerie-masks I created to meet others' ideas of who I should be followed me into college, graduate school, and my career, where it was more of the same. I was pushing myself to excel and be recognized so I could feel acknowledged, accepted and loved. I continued to stuff down my feelings, which filled my heart with painful conflict and made my intuitive voice harder to hear and less clear.

I developed a pattern of over-valuing my head's rational guidance. I had invested a lot in developing my logical, analytical, left-brain. As a result, my choices generally reflected what I *thought* I needed to do to be accepted by others, rather than what my true inner-Self *knew* or wanted. Even when I could feel a suggestion inside that I should move with caution or go completely in a different direction, I questioned it and used rational analysis to make the decision. I wasn't listening to my intuitive inner guidance. This resulted in a pattern of disappointments that made me feel like I could be my own worst enemy.

I was also looking outside of myself for everything I thought I needed to feel whole: belonging, love, acceptance, intimacy, security, happiness—and I was holding everyone in my life responsible for giving it to me. By my mid-thirties I had become an accomplished, driven, drill sergeant of a boss, responding to every situation in life and business like the Marines storm a beach: hard-charging, precision in motion, tough as nails and proud of it. And now, it was *my* way or the highway.

In 2004, after an award-winning, fast-track, corporate ascent, I landed in a Vice President of Marketing role in a $16 billion dollar company, leading a large portfolio of regional and national brands. I was proud to have made it to the pinnacle of my career, and I'd arrived without any idea that I was that close. I felt an inner wariness about the role from the beginning, but I would not allow myself to hear that voice. I rationalized what it would mean for my financial future and career stature to have the title, salary, and validation of my talent, and I accepted the job offer. The old feelings of inadequacy and unworthiness seemed to fade, and briefly, I celebrated finally being seen, heard, understood, and welcomed.

I started this new adventure with bright-eyed excitement. I had dreamed of living in Southern California for years, and now I would be living an *executive's* life there. Nice title, big salary, wonderful perks. I'd worked so hard for the past 20 years, and finally, powerful people were seeing *all* that I had to offer. I was a Black woman at the top! I could finally stop striving and relax into what I was sure would be a fulfilling and happy new chapter in my life.

My mom and dog, Maggie Mae, accompanied me on the cross country drive. I bought a beautiful 3-bedroom, 3-bath condo in a prestigious, guard-gated community in Irvine and settled into a nice rhythm. But what I thought would be a fairytale quickly became my worst nightmare. Personally, I wasn't creating connected and intimate relationships. The knowledge and capability I'd brought with me weren't working as well as they had in my other career roles. I was hired to be a change-agent, but the changes were slow to take hold, and I was impatient. I was used to working independently, but I was feeling micromanaged and unsupported, and sometimes, even sabotaged. The stress got higher as my self-confidence took a nose-dive.

I dug in and worked harder, fighting the fear and resentment welling up inside me, and crying almost every night by the time I made it from my office to my car. I was far from happy, and on several occasions went to sleep expecting to be fired the next day. Even when my boss initiated conversations about my experiences, offering to back me out of the position and help me cut my losses, I plodded on, determined to *make it work*, adamant that I would find a way to demonstrate that I was up to the challenges, and could take whatever was dished out. I didn't know how to do anything else. I was conditioned to suffer through, to grin and bear it, to buck up and get it done. I could not face the idea of quitting. I had no idea then that there was something called self-love that would be the basis for making that choice. In fact, I thought I *was* being true to myself.

Somewhere around the 459th day of agony, which found me in the Hoag Hospital emergency room fearing I was having a heart attack, I was forced to reflect. It was the first time in my life that I actually could say I hated my life. That was a hard feeling to live with. It was compounded by a deep sense of guilt for having it in the first place since I had so much for which to be grateful and happy. What a double-edged sword! There is no way to win with that kind of inner dialog.

As I lay in the examination area, fearing the diagnosis of what was going on with my heart, I heard my voice say within, "Is this it? Is this what my *entire* life is going to be about? Why is this happening? Where the Hell am I?! W*ho* am I, who am I really supposed to be, and what am I here for?!"

Among other things, I considered myself accomplished and successful. But as I lay there, hooked up to machines monitoring my vital signs, I couldn't help but wonder *at what cost?* At what cost was I fighting to make my place in the world? At what cost had I created my identity, and what was underneath it? At what cost was I sacrificing happiness and would it end up being a waste? Flashing through my mind were the stories I'd heard as a girl about how my life would be hard, and that I'd never fully measure up. *Was I making my life hard so I could feel like I was enough?* Was I finding challenges so that when I finally overcame them, I could feel even better about myself? The questions kept coming—the floodgates of introspection had been opened.

I remembered that nagging doubt I'd had in my chest and gut before taking the job. There was a little voice trying to get my attention. I don't remember getting words, but the *feelings* were constriction in my chest, a queasiness in my gut, and some restlessness. I knew at that time a message was trying to be heard, and it felt like it was "stop." It felt as if it was coming from some deep inner place, and it wanted me to know either the position wasn't right for me, or I wasn't right for it.

I connected those feelings to similar messages from my inner guidance, throughout my life. I'd pushed them aside many, many times before, in favor of rationalizations and practicalities, often related to fear of some form of loss: loss of opportunity, security, relationship, money. I was getting glimpses of how often decisions made in fear ended up landing me in struggle, striving and proving. The more I made connections, the more I could see a pattern unfolding. The many times in the many areas of my life that I had made self-abandoning choices were coming into clear view. I realized the one constant in all of these circumstances was me. It would have been convenient to blame someone or something else, and believe me, I'd done that in the past. But this time, I clearly saw that I was the one choosing, and choosing poorly. Ultimately too, I was the one paying the price.

That was a revelation. The day you acknowledge your life is not fulfilling, and also admit that you are responsible, is a day to celebrate. That is a day to jump for joy and dance a jig in the street! That's a day to mark on your calendar and toast every year. It's the first day of your opportunity for liberation. It's the first day of your journey into freedom. I'm talking about freedom from the false self, the stories, the striving, the coping, the surviving, the pushing and the 'just getting by' that you can keep yourself tangled in when your decisions are not from your Highest Self.

I made a conscious decision in the hospital that night that I'd had enough of a life that was successful but unfulfilling. Although I'd already chosen to take personal responsibility for my present predicament, I knew it would take more than that to make my life better. Still, I started with a simple promise to myself: "I want to feel more love and I want to express more joy. I will find a way to give up the ways I hold myself back, beat myself up, and keep myself down."

That commitment to transform everything about me that was making my life so unfulfilling gave me an immediate uplifting—a warmth from inside that spread throughout my body. I knew my life was about to change forever. I had no idea how to do it when I started, but I knew I'd be looking

> **The shift doesn't happen by wanting it to happen. It takes conscious, committed action to live an authentically happy life.**

for the Truth of me—the aspects that I had closed off and was hiding from. You can't hide from this kind of deep inner Truth forever, and once you really see what the hiding is costing and causing you to lose, you won't want to. I have been on a "radical sabbatical" ever since, and have created an amazing, life-giving shift!

I started by exploring the Me below the surface—my identity—in search of a deeper sense of who and what I really am. I traced the memories of pivotal experiences, good and bad, back through time to unearth whatever was below the surface of them. Next, I explored my internal belief system. I wanted to know where I'd first learned the ideas I carried about myself, my relationship to the world and other people, how life works, and where happiness is. Why had I become so disconnected from my heart and feelings, and how was that playing out in my relationships and decision-making? I longed to reconnect with the pieces of myself that I'd left behind, and at the same time, I was also afraid of what I might find that I had run away from. I wondered, would I be able to face it now? I was afraid, sad, and deeply tired a lot. But I wanted to know for sure how and why I was holding myself back.

My days of trusting organized religion for answers had long since gone. But I had always been spiritual, and that's where I turned for support. Through various spiritual workshops, coaches, and books, I was exposed to the ideas of Consciousness and Oneness in ways I'd never internalized them before. I had experiences and revelations that sometimes left me breathless, some taking me months to process. There were peaceful times of feeling like I was making progress, still times that felt like stagnation, and chaotic times that made me fear I had not yet hit rock bottom. There were also peaceful and heart-opening times of knowing that I was safe and loved.

Bit by bit, the spiritual wisdom and committed action paid off. I was piecing together a clearer picture of where I'd gotten the ideas about myself that were running me, but at the same time, in my way. Believe it or not, they date back to my earliest experiences, including some that I believe were imprinted in the womb. No one directly said, "you are unworthy," "the world is not safe," or "you're not lovable." But those stories were inside my idea of myself anyway. I had created them subconsciously in response to things happening around and to me. They became a part of who I thought I was, figments of my imagination and interpretation, and they followed me like a shadow everywhere. They were blocking my True Self from being expressed, and keeping me from the life I desire and deserve.

I believe this is the way it happens for all of us. We pick up subconscious imprinting through the journeys of our lives. It doesn't matter if you move to another state, change schools, leave relationships, give up friends, or accept other jobs, this imprinting will go wherever you go. If it's not in alignment with your Highest Self, it will hold you back. Until you are willing to look below the surface of your identity, behaviors, beliefs, reactions, preferences, and stories to discover what

> **The** process of transforming my shadow self has brought me to a place of rebirth or renaissance.

it is and where it came from, you risk having your life not really be your life. Like me, you will live the life of your shadow self.

The shift doesn't happen by wanting it to happen. It takes conscious, committed action to live an authentically happy life. You must be willing to dismantle the belief system of your shadow self and heal the wounds that created it. Otherwise, you will be blocked from achieving your full potential of peace, love, joy, freedom and abundance, and your Soul—your True Self—will keep calling you until you listen. I now know the trials and tribulations in my life were my Soul's call. *Your* struggles are calling you to realizations about your relationship with yourself, as well. Your struggles are an opportunity to explore how you might be holding yourself back. Will you hear, explore, and act?

The process of transforming my shadow self has brought me to a place of rebirth or renaissance. It's the kind of "born again" to which I can relate. I know in my heart I have different feelings about myself, my experiences, and my place and purpose in the world. My life has a deeper meaning to me, and it feels sweeter than ever before. I wish I had known in my late adolescent years of 15-22 what I know now. I wish I'd been taught about Universal Spiritual Laws and loving myself back then. I would have liked to know how to be in relationship with others and not lose myself. I could have benefitted from being able to see my problems through my Soul's perspective instead of just my ego-based human eyes. I could have contributed more to the world as the Higher version of me. The happiness and success I achieved would have been much deeper and greater.

I developed my **4 Step Living Happy To Be ME!** process to help you rebirth yourself *before* you find yourself in a crisis wondering why your life feels more empty and unfulfilling even when you're working hard to make it so much more. It is my sincere desire to help you release your shadow beliefs and behaviors so you can connect more deeply to your heart, express your Highest Self, and reach your full potential. We unwittingly give life to the shadow self at very young ages, so regardless of whether you're 15 or 50, you can be more happy, successful and fulfilled by living with this process as your foundation. The sooner you start, the better it can be! Regardless of your age, there is guidance for you in these pages. I'm glad you've chosen this book. Thank you for entrusting me with your journey to raise your Consciousness and create a more wonderful life.

I invite you to turn the page now and get started **Living Happy to Be ME!** and *Dancing Your Soul Lightstyle!*

EMBRACE THE TRUTH ABOUT HAPPINESS

Until I was fairly deep into my "radical sabbatical," I used to *chase* happiness ... almost literally. I would flit from one experience to another—workshops, parties, gatherings, friendships, relationships, seminars, vacations—trying to create more happiness in my life. I was confident that if I could just have one more fantastic experience, absorb one more exquisite nugget of knowledge, sort out some aspect of the unknown, tackle another goal, earn another promotion, make more money, or have that great "love of my life," I'd have all the happiness I could ever want. But that's not what happened.

Like so many millions of people around the globe, I was taught that happiness is a result of some form of "doing-ness." From early in our lives, we learn to almost *perform* for it, as though it's a reward for having done something nice or right, like the treats I used to give my dog Maggie Mae when she was a particularly good girl. And so, many of us do our *own* form of "tricks." We strive, accomplish, and excel. We make sacrifices, focus on others, and chase experiences. We ignore emotions, push hurts away, and pretend that everything is "fine."

In fact, there *are* some great times when we really do feel good. There are moments when we're absolutely sure we've found the happiness prize and life *is* better. Let's check-in on how this has worked in your life. Pause in your reading and play with the questions on the next couple of pages about your relationship with happiness.

Check-in

What are your beliefs about happiness, where it comes from/how to have it? Use the next page to write these things down. These answers will be a foundation for the other Check-ins and exercises throughout the book. Be as exhaustive in your answers as possible. You can also come back and add to them later.

What I was taught about happiness and what it should be: Include what your parents said would bring happiness, or what you heard as social or cultural values about happiness that you adopted. Also capture whatever you learned should be your ways to have happiness.

_____
_____
_____
_____
_____
_____
_____
_____
_____
_____
_____
_____
_____
_____
_____
_____
_____
_____
_____

My Definition of happiness is: This is just about you and your ideas and desires relative to happiness.

_____
_____
_____
_____
_____
_____
_____
_____
_____
_____

Next, let's create a Happiness Map. First, make a list of all the things that make you happy. You can get some ideas from the examples below the map on the next page.

_____
_____
_____
_____
_____
_____
_____
_____
_____
_____
_____
_____
_____
_____
_____
_____

Things in Life that Make Me Happy

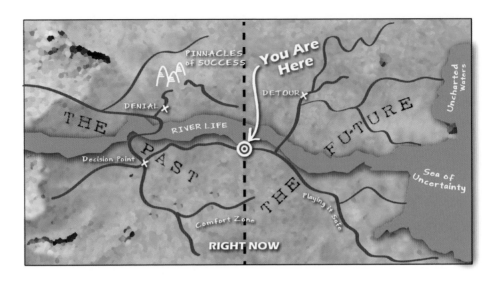

Ideas:

Lose 15 lbs	Finish a project	New baby
Fall in love	Get in shape	Kids going to college
Take a vacation	Get married	Meet the right partner
Win the lottery	Get a divorce	Make more $$$
Get promoted	Find my purpose	Financial independence
Sell the house	Go to church	Buy a house
Get rid of illness	Buy a new car	Volunteer
Spend time in nature	Find a job	Coach a team
Meditate	Become debt-free	Visit relatives
Learn to cook	Start a new hobby	Learn to play an instrument

Now Draw an X in the blank space provided on the next page and write "I'm here" with the date and time. Then put spots on the map for the locations of your happiness relative to where you are today. These are your happiness "destinations." Like a road map, draw the route between you and your happiness destinations.

My Happiness Map:

Now reflect on what you have created. What are the contents of your list and map? How many of your happiness destinations depend on something happening in the future? How many depend on what others do? Were there destinations in the past, and how long did you feel the happiness from those destinations? How far away did you put the closest destination? How long are the journeys to your happiness destinations? Are you in any of the destinations right now? Capture a few thoughts and feelings about your map and your ideas about happiness and keep them as a reference for the exploration we'll be doing later in the book.

_____

_____

_____

_____

_____

_____

_____

_____

_____

_____

If you're like most people, your map has lots of external, achievement-oriented things that are set way out in the future. You may also have destinations that depend on the "others" in your life—children, spouse, business partner, love interest, landlord, neighbors, or others. You probably have things that aren't even in your realm of control, like things under the influence of the economy or the government.

I have no doubt that your life has had wonderful and happy moments. I hope you've had plenty of feel good times when you were absolutely sure you'd found the happiness prize and life *was* better. However, I know you would not be reading this book if those times had lasted. And that's the thing with this externally-driven form of happiness. As time goes by, you realize that the happiness is gone, and like the hamster on its wheel, you set out in search of it once more. You can literally run yourself ragged trying to "find" it again, and again, and again.

We choose careers for security instead of pleasure. We stay in relationships that don't work because it's easier than dealing with the fall-out of leaving. We smile on the outside rather than let people see we are sad or afraid on the inside. We *give* love to *get* love instead of just for the pleasure of loving. We create identities and personalities to mask what we think others won't accept about us, or what we can't accept about ourselves. As a result, we become successful, yet empty; wealthy, yet poor in spirit; renowned, yet unfulfilled. We advance in our careers and get nowhere in our lives. Why, for so many, does the pursuit of happiness end up feeling empty and sad?

We're looking for happiness in all the wrong places!

The external nature of the paradigm we were taught is holding us back. The old DO-HAVE-BE paradigm for deriving happiness teaches that it comes from success, security or some other external end result. We get energized in the here-and-now by the promise of something happening to us or for us (outside of us) at some distant point in the future. In other words, we live for a deferred experience of being happy that is an end-state resulting from other conditions. For example, we DO things (work hard, sacrifice, give to others) to HAVE success (accomplishments/titles/money/prestige/a spouse/cool stuff) so we can BE happy (feel fulfilled/lighter/successful).

Again, the feel-good only lasts as long as the external HAVE condition remains exciting. When that changes, so does the level of feel-good associated with it. When your A-student self gets a B, you may not think there's anything to be happy about. When your dream house becomes too expensive to live in, the happiness related to it turns to sorrow, and maybe even guilt and shame. Sometimes, the relationship doesn't work out, you don't get accepted to the school you want, you don't make the team, you lose the job, or some other result that would be a big YUCK! on the happiness scale happens. The happiness you once associated with the HAVE result is no longer attainable.

This can happen over and over, but somehow, you stay caught in this unfulfilling cycle of happiness. I believe it's because we confuse happiness with excitement. The dictionary defines excitement as "a feeling of great enthusiasm and eagerness."

Excitement is not something that can be sustained forever. It goes up and down depending on the stimulus. You know excitement is a fleeting experience, and what you really want is a way to feel happiness all the time. It's clear the old model isn't serving you.

It's time for a paradigm shift!

Fortunately, there's a higher and deeper way to experience happiness. This kind of happiness is not conditional—meaning it isn't about accomplishments, romantic engagement, pleasing the parents, career progression, financial status, or a retirement plan. This kind of happiness is not a land, off in the distance, to which you must journey. It's not in an amazing experience with your friends. It can't be found in a great orgasm, or a 27-year marriage. It's not awaiting you in some recognition or achievement.

"Then *where is it?!*" you ask.

Once you stop looking in all those external places, there's only one place to turn. In fact, looking outside of yourself for happiness is like a fish swimming around in search of water. The fish is moving in, through and around the water at all times. There's no need for it to search for water. It's the same for you. True and lasting happiness is already a part of who you *really* are, and therefore, available to you every minute. Joy—the deepest and most free experience of happiness—is within your Divine Essence, which is the spiritual nature of you that is having the human experience of your life. This is your Highest Self or your Highest Consciousness. The longer you look for happiness in things outside of this aspect of you, the longer you'll be **UN**fulfilled and **UN**happy.

Moving in, through, and around happiness like a fish swimming in water means you can "Be Happy" all the time. You simply must choose to stay in alignment with the Divine nature of yourself. This means you also release who you are **not** (the shadow self with its masks). When you shift into continually choosing to express the *Divine* nature of yourself, you will *flow* the Divine aspects of yourself into your life. These include Peace, Love, Freedom, and **JOY**, which I feel as a deep and abiding state of happy.

Then what happens is you go from expecting to have a happy or an unhappy life to higher ground. You choose to experience all the situations in your life from the energy of inner happiness. You tap into your Divine nature no matter what is going on around you, and the feelings of joy can flow in you even when your life appears to be full of things you would never associate with traditional ideas of happiness.

Defining *Authentic* Happiness

This is my general definition of *Authentic* Happiness, which I just described above.

> True Happiness is to experience all manner of worldly sorrow, pain, or loss, and still be Joyful in your heart.

This kind of happiness exists regardless of external experiences that we would probably all characterize as **UN**happy. There is no co-dependency in this kind of happiness. It's not a 'hills and valleys' kind of happiness. When you're feeling the True Happiness I describe above, life takes on an indefatigable quality—you can feel more peaceful and fulfilled no matter what is going on around you. You can find yourself smiling on the inside in the midst of not so wonderful experiences happening on the outside. Your sense of 'all is well' is constant no matter what.

How is that possible?

How is it possible to be happy when you're experiencing a tough time in your family, you're struggling with the dynamics of school, or you're facing job loss, physical illness, relationship difficulties, having your car towed, bills piling up and so on? Where does this kind of happiness come from? It's simple really. It comes from elevating your Consciousness and living as an integrated Spiritual-human person. It comes from shifting from an outer awareness and focus to an inner one.

Living Happy To Be ME! is an inside game. It's about you and what's going on inside you. Only that. No more building happiness on outside experiences. They can shift too quickly and easily, and they are outside your realm of control. This is the proverbial house built on sand. When those external things shift, so does your opportunity for happiness. Whenever you give up responsibility for what you *can* create, you simultaneously give away your power *to* create. In order to have the kind of life you desire, you have to be willing to focus on being the conscious co-creator of that life. Are you consciously creating or are you waiting for things to happen in your favor?

Is your focus on you, or on someone or something else?

Check-in

Here's an opportunity to consider another important question. Where is your primary focus in your life: on you or on others? To help you decide, go back and peruse your happiness list and map, and notice how many things were external. Then ask yourself, "Why?" At what points in your past and from what situations did you learn to make your experience of happiness about what other people did or what external circumstances were showing up? How many other things in your life are externally generated? In other words, how often do you do things to please others, placate others, and/or fit-in with others?

It's *critical* for you to get clear on this, so continue to ask the question internally until you get clarity.

Where is my focus?

I focus on pleasing me when...

_____

_____

_____

I focus on pleasing others when...

_____

_____

_____

_____

_____

_____

_____

_____

It didn't take me very long to see how many of my decisions were about pleasing others rather than myself. I think we all can point to the things we do for parents, siblings, children and spouses. We want them to think well of us and do good by us in return, and so we can often make our desires secondary to pleasing them. From choosing what college to attend, what major to select, what career to pursue, who to marry and when, where to live, and on and on, many people are subconsciously being run by things that keep them focused on everything and everyone *but* themselves. The kids, spouse, career, charity organization, church, sports team, and multiple other responsibilities and commitments get their focus and love. Except for meeting *others'* needs and expectations, they are not truly in the equation— meaning they are not truly in their own lives.

An example of this is how many men lose themselves in their careers. They become focused on it as the means through which they create prosperity, fun, stability, and peace in their lives—which generally also means in the lives of their family members. In too many cases, what you feel when you dig a little deeper is that the career-focused or workaholic men don't really *love* their jobs or working so hard. Yet they continue to do it because they believe people are counting on them, and they don't want to let those people down. Their sense of self-worth has gotten entangled with a learned aspect of identity for men, like 'bread-winner,' 'provider,' or 'protector.'

These men may not be aware, but like me, they are wearing masks to make it all look nice and neat on the outside. Instead of leading to happiness, this turns into self-sacrifice that creates heartache and sadness, and potentially emotional resentment and physical illness. The same can be true for women strongly identified with the role of mother, who create their entire existence in service to their children. Then when the role shifts as the children leave the nest, the mother role gets interrupted or in some cases is over altogether, and the mother has no idea who or how to be. The shift in the outer circumstance creates major disconnection and distress on the inside as she figures out how to be herself in her own life. It is not necessary to have this kind of internal disruption every time there is an external change.

Happiness is a part of who you are!

True happiness—Joy—is our innate State of Being. It's an immutable aspect of who we are as Divine Spiritual Beings. We incarnate in the world into human bodies, but our essential nature is not *of* this world. That True Essence is Peaceful, Joyful and Free when we first enter this world. Then, over time, we are taught separation: the concept of a Divine Creator *outside* of us and completely *separate* from us. We gradually get conditioned to disconnect from this Higher Consciousness aspect of ourselves. We have an experience, feel a sensation, observe a situation, deduce a meaning, and connect that meaning to who we are, what we're capable of and why we're here. We become more and more *OF* this world, meaning we lose the internal awareness of ourselves as Divine Beings, and along with that awareness goes the power to co-create our lives consciously.

There are lots of ways for this to happen. Let's look at the primary reason right now by exploring an ages-old question. Which is more important…your head or your heart?

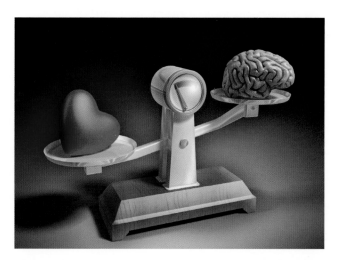

This was difficult for me to answer for myself because I was a walking, talking HEAD—a powerful thinker and analyzer who loved to know things. A "TJ" in Myer's Briggs terminology. I thought I was experiencing and expressing feelings, but in general, I was pretty mental…analytical, intellectual, and rational. I tended to talk *about* my feelings without really experiencing or allowing myself to outwardly express them. Often, I wasn't talking about feelings at all. I was sharing judgments—what was right/wrong, good/bad, and better/worse. Judgments come from the head—the conscious mind, as it does its job of comparing, measuring, and analyzing.

Our heads are very important to how we move through, survive, and thrive in our world. We need the head's ability to sort, process, and analyze information and its ability to assess, calculate, memorize, and compare data. But when the head works alone, it can create distorted perspectives, resulting in stressful thoughts and emotions. These include judgment of self and others, envy, resentment, worry, guilt, shame, blame, anger, and what I believe is the most powerful yet subtle: fear. These are the by-products of the head's non-stop comparison, assessment, and analysis run amuck, without the wider intuitive understanding of the heart.

Your head holds your belief systems, values, and standards. It uses these as the litmus test against which it compares everything you encounter. You see something and in milliseconds, you have a judgment about it. This is not necessarily bad. If you are aware of the underlying driver in your head that triggered the response, you at least know the source of the dynamic. However, sometimes, your beliefs are buried; you are not really conscious of them.

Paramahansa Yogananda talks about the potential for the judgments of the rational mind to send us astray in his book *The Yoga of Jesus*: "Human Knowledge filters in through the senses and is interpreted by the mind. If the senses err in perception, the conclusion drawn by the understanding of that data is also incorrect."

For example, unbeknownst to me throughout much of my life, my head was filled with lack and limitation thinking, and ideas of being inadequate, unworthy, and unlovable that I had picked up very early in my life. I never made a conscious choice to value lack or attach to limitation, and I certainly *never* made a conscious declaration of "I'm unworthy! I'm not enough!, or I'm unlovable!" Nor did anyone in my life directly "teach" me that I was. But the little girl mind created an erring perception of herself, and over time, it gave life to negative beliefs, giant icebergs, hiding beneath the surface of my expression in the world. I was subconsciously being run by them as I created coping behaviors through my personality, identity and masks of confidence, drive, poise, intelligence, happiness and charm. Here's how the cause-effect looks in a table:

Subconscious False Beliefs (My Head's Perspective)	Reflection in My Life
I must work harder than others to be seen, heard, understood, valued and loved.	I was competitive and aggressive, intent on having the world measure me based on what I was capable of instead of my gender or the color of my skin. I chose difficult paths, attracted difficult relationships, and tried to do everything myself to prove I could get it done without help. I looked driven and accomplished, but I was running mostly on fear and resentment. People experienced me as controlling, aggressive and angry.

Subconscious False Beliefs (My Head's Perspective)	Reflection in My Life
Family/friends/experiences/achievements will make me happy.	Happiness was elusive, and never filled me up. I was a loyal, generous, selfless friend; yet often felt like people were "letting me down" or taking advantage of me. People experienced me as demanding and self-centered.
My value in the world is determined by my business titles, material wealth, associates, knowledge, and things that I own.	Constant chase for professional and personal success, but rarely if ever feeling fulfillment.
Intellect is more valued than emotions. People will only really see me if I show them my intellect.	I pushed to prove my knowledge, needing to be right about everything. I hated questions because I thought people were using them to prove that I *didn't* know much. I attracted people who were emotionally unavailable. I did not feel comfortable and safe being emotionally intimate.
I need to please others and my needs/desires don't count.	I felt like I always did more in relationships. I attracted people I needed to take care of. People took from, and then often abandoned me. I abandoned myself in order to have others love me.

I've learned that at the heart of all that matters, is the heart—the intuitive, sacred wisdom of the heart, our *emotional* intelligence system. Your heart holds the Divine Truth of you—that you are much more than human, yet human nonetheless. I believe that in the Divine energy of the heart is the Soul, the very root of the Divinity that you are. The part of you that is on Earth even as you are in Heaven. The aspect that is immortal and eternal. The pure Consciousness that is not of this world, but just passing through it by way of an "earth-suit" called the body. At any moment in time, you are individually expressing your human-influenced variations of a Universal Being-ness born of the Heavens, descended into Earth, one with God as "Image and Likeness" and therefore, not the creation of the experiences of this world, but a higher expression altogether. You are an individuated expression of that which is omnipresent, omniscient, expanding, light-upon-light, and love unconditional. We all are.

My heart remained full of the **Magnificent Essence** that is my birthright as this Divine Spiritual Being, in spite of what I'd learned and carried in my head. This inner Divine Truth or Essence of me was always available to me to access and live from. It kept calling me, but I was so disconnected that I barely heard, and when I did, I often didn't trust it enough to listen and follow its guidance. What I mean when I say 'disconnected' is that I didn't allow myself to really feel or express my true feelings or purest intentions. They would try to come up from within, but I had learned to stuff them back down again. So they had no outlet, and I became numb to their impulses. This doesn't mean they are not there. Are you able to remember times when you might have felt this kind of disconnection within? Happiness can be experienced incessantly when you can tap into and stay connected with this aspect of yourself. You can allow yourself to feel and flow whatever unhappy or difficult feelings come to you, and then release them, and shift from that lower experience to tune back in to your Higher Consciousness that was and always will be there. I believe this is about expressing through the emotional heart.

In the end though, it's not about one or the other, head OR heart. It's really about both.

Living Happy to Be ME! is about leading with the heart and integrating the head.

Here's why. Scientific research by the Institute of Heart Math has proven the power in the heart. Their data shows there is an electrical field surrounding the physical heart that is a source of higher intelligence. In fact, IHS says it's 60 times stronger than the electrical field of the brain, which is also a source of higher intelligence. Core heart feelings of love, care, compassion, tolerance, patience, forgiveness, gratitude, and kindness are the root of this "heart intelligence." When you are tuned-in, you can more easily discern what you desire and make better choices for fulfilling experiences. It's like a radio dial. The music is always there at station 105.9, but you will never hear it when your dial is tuned in to the station at 88.7.

So if the messages at 88.7 are the ego-based, rational, subconscious, judgment and intellect-driven chatter of the head, you must choose to re-tune your dial into the compassionate, tolerant and unconditional guidance of the heart. You must up-level your focus from safety, security and power to connectedness, Oneness and Unconditional Love. Raising your Consciousness then becomes an ongoing practice of quieting your head while opening and tuning into your heart. There is an inner knowingness in your heart that is speaking to you at all times. The more you actively access this heart intelligence or heart power, the more you strengthen your intuitive sense of direction. When you live your life from this higher aspect of you, while integrating the more rational wisdom of the head, you can reach your highest potential and fulfill your dreams—and you can do it more fluidly. According to the Institute of Heart Math, when you tune into the frequency of your heart in concert with the wisdom of your head, you can reprogram and harmonize your entire mental and emotional nature to bring balance and fulfillment. Think of the mind working as a sub-terminal for non-cognitive intelligence coming from the heart. Albert Einstein said it like this:

The intuitive mind is a sacred gift and the rational mind, its faithful servant. We have created a society that worships the servant and has forgotten the gift.

~ Albert Einstein

How exciting to have one who is recognized as among the world's most-brilliant scientists advocating intuition as your primary guiding force! Time for another quick check-in. I know that when I look back on some of the so-called "disasters" in my life, after honest assessment, I realize how often I went with my head over my heart. This was not because my heart wasn't giving me a clear message. In fact, my heart was clearly saying yes or no, but my head was doing its thing: weighing options, playing devil's advocate, running fear-based scenarios, etc. In the end, I often steered myself away from my heart's directions feeling like the rational was more concrete and true.

When I advocate giving priority to the inner heart, I'm not talking about romance, nor am I talking about you becoming a "softie." I'm talking about being willing to trust your inner knowingness above your intellectual assessment for the "WHAT?" decisions, and then leveraging your rational, intellectual, knowledge-based self for the "HOW?" decisions—while also keeping room open for Divine Intelligence to 'weigh in' for that too. For example, when I was making career choice decisions in high school, I could feel an inner pulling toward something that felt expansive energetically, but my head always put things in terms of where I'd find the most security and prestige fastest. Over and over, I didn't pursue what I felt was calling me at a more emotional level. Interestingly, two of those things are part of my experience now: teaching and carrying a message to many (broadcaster).

> You'll never be able to escape from your heart. So it's better to listen to what it has to say. ~ Paolo Coelho

Check-in

It's helpful to notice how this has played out in your own experience. Can you discern the difference between your head's intellect and your heart's intuitive guidance talking? Let's check-in on that right now. Close your eyes and take a couple of deep breaths. Allow your body and mind to relax, and allow yourself to come to stillness within. Open yourself to an awareness of your intuitive voice and how it speaks to you. Allow yourself to get in touch with times when you could feel it sharing guidance. Have there been times when you could sense a knowingness within? When you feel your answer building inside you, open your eyes and capture as many of the situations, sensations, feelings and messages below.

Hearing My Heart-Wisdom

Times I have heard/felt my heart guiding me:

_____

_____

_____

_____

_____

_____

_____

_____

_____

_____

_____

Now with these situations, sensations, and messages in mind, write below about how your head responded. Close your eyes and take a couple of deep breaths. Allow your body and mind to relax, and allow yourself to get back to stillness within. Open yourself to an awareness of your head's voice and how it speaks to you. Allow yourself to get in touch with the times and ways it shares guidance. Have there been times when the head argued with or discounted your inner knowingness? When you feel your answer building inside you, open your eyes and capture as many of the situations, sensations, feelings and messages below.

Times I have heard/felt my head guiding me:

_____

_____

_____

_____

_____

_____

_____

_____

_____

Now with the answers above, see if you can get a sense of the contrasts. In the table below, capture any awareness of how the heart speaks to you that is different from how the head speaks to you. How does their respective guidance feel? Where do you sense it? Which feels better? Does one feel more True or Real to you? See if you can sum major ideas into single word answers.

When my heart speaks, I am aware of:	When my head speaks, I am aware of:

What are you noticing? Right now, is your heart giving you a knowingness about this exercise that your head is arguing with or discounting? If that is happening, you are not alone. I have worked with people from 15-80 years of age who all tell me the same thing—once they allow themselves to consciously notice, they can connect to major differences between these two voices, and how their guidance feels and sounds. Next is what I've captured over time, from my personal exploration and counseling clients, to characterize these differences. Can you see similarities between what you wrote and what is in the chart on the next page?

Tendencies of Heart Intelligence	Tendencies of Head Intelligence
Playful and Fun: How do I have pleasure in this moment? What feels good? How do I access and express the joy within? Will this help me laugh and play more?	**Rational and Analytical:** What is the cost of this choice versus that one? How do I live up to others' expectations? How do I win or cut my losses? How will I look or be perceived?
Expansive: How is there more for all? What more is possible than what I'm experiencing now? Can this help me achieve my highest potential? What is in the highest and best for all concerned?	**Contracting:** There is only so much to go around. I should be careful wanting or asking for too much. What are the rules in this situation and how can I not violate them? It's not safe to be too big or ask for too much.
Tolerant: How do I accept you, connect with you, and experience our similarities? How can I allow you to have your own experiences even if they are different from mine? What can I learn from or experience with you even though I'm not exactly like you?	**Hierarchical and Competitive:** How do I define myself as better than or worse than you? How do I see myself as more than the good that you are and less than the bad that you are? How do I top you and/or keep you from topping me?
Compassionate: I feel your pain, fear, and inadequacy, as much as I can feel my own. I'm sorry you are feeling it. How can I support or help you? How can I lighten your load?	**Self-Interested:** How do I get you to see, hear, and understand me more than you see, hear or understand others? How do I get what I want/need from you? How do I get you to alleviate my pain? How do I get you to take care of me?
In Oneness: I see you in me. I feel you as me. I hear my voice in yours. I want the best for you as I want the best for me. I am you and you are me.	**In Separation:** I am different from you and you are different from me. This is mine and that is yours. I am here and you should be over there. These are my things and those are yours.
Loving: I am being love. I flow love to you without conditions and I receive love from you without conditions. Love is the end goal of all I do and the totality of what I am.	**Fearful:** What do I risk by associating with you? What will you do to me if I am vulnerable with you? What will you do to me if I show weakness? How badly will I be hurt if I let you win or let you in?

What I have come to know is that my heart speaks as the deeper aspect of me that is the True Self. This is what the capital **M E** in **Living Happy To Be ME!**, stands for: **Magnificent Essence.** I use it interchangeably with Higher Consciousness, Soul, and Divine Nature. It's your Spiritual core—the central and foundational aspect of *what* you are. This Essence is your Divine Beingness of Peace, Love, Freedom, and Joy. At the deepest level, these are the things you seek from your life, yet they were instilled in you before you got here, and they are available to you every moment you are here. Your Peaceful, Joyful, Loving and Free nature is here to guide you through the experiences of your life, rather than be the end result you strive for as you "do" life.

This Earth-bound life is supposed to be about growing into a deeper realization of this Truth through the choices you make as your life unfolds. In this way, your life is an opportunity to continually claim Truth over false beliefs, Love over fear, Freedom over attachment to what doesn't serve you, and Happiness over struggle, anger, guilt, blame, shame, and punishment. You are not trying to fix a broken version of yourself. In fact, I don't believe there is such a thing.

All unhappiness, all strife, all pain, all unwanted experiences are reflections of an inner state that is calling to you to be adjusted. There's never any piece or part missing from inside of you—or anyone else. What's missing is the connection to or alignment with your **Magnificent Essence.** What's missing is an integration and embodiment of the *Divine Nature* with the humanness. This integrated Spiritual-Human is what you are here to express. One who walks as the Truth and Light of Heaven while living an earthly experience.

But this is only possible through conscious choice, also known as free will. You must *choose* to bring forth into your life the True totality of who and what you are. You can not choose what you are unwilling to believe exists. So the first Step in the process to embody the **Living Happy To Be ME!** Lightstyle is to fully **Wake Up!** to this Truth.

What is this precious love and laughter
Budding in our Hearts?

It is the Glorious Sound
Of a Soul Waking Up!

~ Hafiz

Embody the Four Steps of
Living Happy To Be ME!

Step 1: Wake Up! To the Truth of You

We are now, we have always been, and we will always be the eternal, unlimited Self (God). All we need to do is to realize that by removing the ignorance of it, or by increasing our knowingness of it. ~ Lester Levenson

As I began to review the history of the journey of my life, I gradually realized how asleep-at-the-wheel I had been. I had been going through the motions of living, getting by on bits of excitement between periods of loneliness, struggle, resentment, and sadness. I'm talking about the money, social life, wine, food, vacations, and other deliverers of short-lived, sensory pleasure. I think of them as "false elixirs of feel-good," and I'd become attached to them, and thought they were the real happiness I was seeking. This sense-happiness made my life more palatable. I discovered how much my identity was based on past experiences that were lodged in my subconscious mind, keeping me in a sort of dream state.

I used to go to parties and events and feel alone in the midst of people I called good friends. I got accolades, won awards and received promotions, and still felt like I had to do more and more to look good at my job or hang onto anything I had achieved. I was an accomplished soccer player and sprinter, yet the big personal victories seemed elusive. I used to feel like I had to constantly push the men in my life to prove how much they cared about or loved me without seeing I'd attracted men who couldn't.

Even though I felt my life was really, really good almost all the time on the surface, deep down, there was a restlessness, a disbelief, a *questioning*. I could feel that there must be more fulfillment to experience, but whenever I went after it the way I had been doing it in the past, it felt more elusive. I started to feel like my life would be a never-ending series of *"almosts,"* and that I couldn't truly have what I wanted most. In fact, I wasn't really sure I knew what I wanted, but I knew it felt harder and harder to get it.

> As you be the Joy that you are, there is more Joy on the planet.

If within you right now you feel even a tiny bit of resonance with what I'm describing, it's no accident that you're reading this book. Whatever you're seeing as your wake-up call, know that it's your Higher Consciousness trying to get your attention. Don't wait until you end up in a hospital thinking you're having a heart attack like I did, or until you experience something worse. Starting exactly where you are right now, just say "Yes!" to going on this journey into you. Say "Yes!" to taking the blinders off and going beyond the 'way it's always been.' Say "Yes!" to getting below the surface of your life experiences by engaging in an "archeology of the self." *Dig deep* into everything you think you hold dear in your life. Every aspect of your personality and identity, especially the parts that you are absolutely sure are the real you, should be open to new scrutiny.

Allow your inner knowingness to help you uncover and surrender whatever you've picked up over time as part of your coping behaviors. Listen for the messages about what is no longer serving you in your life, and take steps to make new choices that help you spiral up into a more awakened, empowered, authentic, peaceful and joyful you. Awaken to the perfection you already are and always have been! That is the you that you really want to express, and that's the you the world is waiting for.

By being more of your Essence, you bring more light and love into the world, and it creates a ripple effect that touches multitudes for the better.

As you be the Peace that you are, there is more Peace on the planet. As you be the Love that you are, there is more Love on the planet. As you be Free from the fears of the false self, there is more Freedom on the planet. As you be the Joy that you are, there is more Joy on the planet. As you awaken to the perfection that you already are, striving ceases and you will feel a fullness within you with your life exactly as it is, in all ways and always. You will have opened yourself up to receive every gift, every abundance in the Universe!

Check-in

Close your eyes, take a deep breath and allow yourself to feel that within. Sit with these words in your mind for a few minutes: "I AM already everything I need to be to feel fulfilled and happy."

Wake Up! to the Truth of You is the first action Step to living the integrated **Living Happy To Be ME!** Lightstyle. It's more about remembering something you already know deep within, than learning something new with your intellect. It's about remembering that you are a Spiritual being experiencing a human realm, reconnecting and realigning with your Essence. Awakening provides an opportunity for rebirth—one where you are born into the world again, and you get to parent yourself through the rest of your life, making choices and experiencing connection from a place of Divine Truth and Light, rather than from the expression of the mighty ego and the fears and sadnesses from the past.

As you fully realize your Divinity, you create enormous potential to right all perceived wrongs, overcome all perceived obstacles, and transcend all perceived past hurts. But realization is just the beginning. The real shift happens when you take the knowingness into action—when you *embody* this Truth in every aspect of your life.

The embodiment is about fully being everything you already are. Think of the relationship of a wave with the ocean. Every wave is a reflection of the full majesty of the whole ocean simply by being what it already is—the ocean expressing as a wave. We don't look at the wave and say, "That's just a wave. It's not really the ocean." The tiniest acorn has the full measure of the great oak tree within it. The foundational Eastern spiritual viewpoint is that God lives within us and that our essential nature *is* God. The Vedanta, Baghavad Gita and other sacred Eastern texts teach that the *Atma*, or Supreme Self, is truly who we are, and that this Divine energy exists in everything and everyone. The Western religious view is largely that man is separate from God and different from the nature of God. But there is evidence in the Christian tradition that oneness with God is Truth. It can be found in how you interpret the messages of perhaps Christianity's most revered figure.

While many believe he was demonstrating what was unique to him as Savior, others believe the great Hebrew Master known as Jesus taught about and demonstrated the inner Divinity of man—the Oneness with the Divinity of God. References in the Bible's collection of words attributed to Jesus reflect this belief. My two favorites are from John 10:30, "I and the Father are one." and John 14:20, "I am in my Father, and you in me, and I in you." For me, the whole idea of man created as "Image and Likeness," means that you have the full measure of God-nature or Divinity within you. I believe Jesus came to help us reconnect to and align with that nature of us *within*. And what better way to do it than to demonstrate it while incarnated as a human.

He said we are to enter the Kingdom of God, which is "within you." His message was about how to achieve, as a human, a higher experience of life—how to transcend life as a mere mortal, trapped in sensory perception, and limited by earthly knowledge and materiality.

What I'm talking about and what I believe Jesus, and all ascended Spiritual Masters came to show us, is the Highest Consciousness that *we* are, not the Highest Consciousness that *they* were. They taught the deeper Universal science that underlies religious dogma. They provided us with practices to become vessels for the all-knowing, ever-present, ever-expanding Divine Principle of Life, Light and Love to express on Earth.

As you re-awaken your awareness of this Divine nature within, you become a more full expression of it. You become able to demonstrate the transcendent nature of Divine Life while you walk as a human. You will remember the underlying Divine nature of all things, and how all is interrelated in a great web of existence. Your life experiences will contribute to the greater web and the greater web will contribute to you. As your life reflects the Higher Consciousness that you are expressing, you get to experience Heaven *while you are on Earth*.

Your acknowledgement of yourself as this Essence is critical to all of this taking place. Importantly too, you must go beyond an intellectual or mind level relationship with this Truth. The messages, miracles, and mysteries that you have experienced in your life that *cannot* be explained by knowledge and logic are here to help you.

They are a reminder that there is much more to your Earthly existence than what you can describe with your five senses. They are inviting you to go from being attached to a body-Consciousness, to integrating your spiritually-enlightened Consciousness. Then you will be able to truly understand and know what is going on around you and why. Then you will be able to figure out the part you are here to play.

This transformation is what I meant in the previous section when I said I felt like I was reborn. It's how you are "born again" into an awake and aware experience of your Divine Soul-Being Self while walking in human form via the vessel called the physical body. This is the experience of yourself as an aspect of the 'I Am' Consciousness that gave life to all things.

The Ego

What gets in the way of being able to have this rebirth is the ego. What comes to mind when you think about your ego? For the purpose of a spiritual discussion, these two Google Dictionary definitions of ego feel most appropriate:

- The part of the mind that mediates between the conscious and the unconscious and is responsible for reality testing and a sense of personal identity.

- The Self: your Consciousness of your own identity.

In his book, *The Power of Intention*, Wayne Dyer talks about the ego being a "speck in the ocean that thinks it's the entire ocean." Eckhart Tolle defines ego in his book, *The Power of Now* like this:

> *"As you grow up, you form a mental image of who you are, based on your personal and cultural conditioning. We may call this phantom self the ego. It consists of mind activity and can only be kept going through continuous thinking."*

The term ego means different things to different people, but when I use it here it means a false self, created by unconscious identification with the mind. To the ego, the present moment hardly exists. Only past and future are its focus, and it tends to keep you focused there as well. It is concerned with keeping the past alive, because without it, you question who you are.

Do you feel yourself wanting certain things today primarily or even solely because in the past, they were somehow pleasing? Do you similarly avoid certain things today for the same reason—you don't want to relive something about them that you remember from your past experience of them? Ego constantly projects itself into the future to ensure its continued survival and to seek some kind of release or fulfillment *there*. The ego says: "One day, when this, that or the other happens, I am going to be okay, happy, at peace."

In fact however, the present moment is where all of life is. Your only opportunity to live is in the single instant unfolding for you right now. If you cannot be you, fully present and fully empowered to express and make choices in *this* moment, your life can only be a series of repeat performances of the past, while you prepare for the future. This is not how you were meant to express your Magnificence in your life. Ego's total reversal of the Truth shows how, when in ego mode, we humans can be wildly dysfunctional.

I think of ego as the limited idea I have of myself that is formed from my existence. It's the lower case m e. The equation is:

$$\begin{array}{ll} \textbf{My personality} & + \\ \textbf{My identity} & + \\ \textbf{The monetary and emotional} & \\ \textbf{value of my "stuffology"} & + \\ \underline{\textbf{My "woundology"}} & \underline{=} \\ \qquad\qquad \textbf{me} & \end{array}$$

When you're in the 'asleep-at-the-wheel of your life' state that I mentioned earlier, you don't recognize this aspect of yourself as a separate entity. Even if you're wealthy, healthy, and wise, ego's influence is keeping you feeling you are *less* of everything. You don't realize that it has power over how you behave and choose. You think it *is* you. When you start to step back and ponder questions like "what aspect of me is having this thought, or entertaining that idea?" you start to separate from the ego and enable yourself to delve deeper into who and what you *really* are.

This delving is the beginning of the **Wake Up!** Step. It started for me in the emergency room that day when I thought I was having a heart attack. It happens for many people that way: near-death experiences, life-threatening diseases, loss of loved ones or fortunes, the proverbial "dark night of the Soul." Why is crisis so often the catalyst for this kind of in-depth questioning of ourselves? Because crisis forces us to focus on what and how we are creating our experiences. Crisis forces us to take a pause from the past and future to focus on what is happening in the present moment. Crisis brings the world we *think* we know to a screeching halt.

> *You can't create a great life if you choose to stay asleep-at-the-wheel of the unfulfilling life you're already living.*

Crisis can also make you get beyond the previous blocks that kept you from going below the surface. There can be no more "ostriching"—hiding your head in the sand, pretending you can't hear your Divine Nature calling you. You are almost slapped into awakening—offered an opportunity to confront fears, explore angers, and recall disappointments. You tackle what is presenting itself in the present moment that makes you question more deeply why you're here, and why certain things are happening, and others are not. Many people have more than one such opportunity in their lifetimes, but they pass through them unaware. In fact, the most powerful aspect of the **Wake Up!** may very well be that you notice you're at such a crossroads.

For the **Wake Up!** to be complete, you must claim a knowingness about being *more* than the ego would have you believe you are. You do that by creating a deeper relationship with yourself. I believe my Purpose in my life is to teach about the power of this relationship. Self-awareness, self-acceptance and self-love are what I have come to know as the keys to the kingdom of Heaven on Earth. The more you empower yourself from the inside out, the greater your experience of the life you are yearning to create. From the place of knowing Self, you can evaluate how you "show up," which helps you identify what in your engagement with life is Divine in nature, and what is ego. Ego is the "not Self" or "false-self," and as you get clear on the aspects of your being and doingness that fall into association with ego, you can distinguish from that what is associated with the Divine.

The thing is, most people don't typically invest time in knowing themselves better or deeper. I have always considered myself pretty self-aware, and even so, until I did a purposeful dive into my history, there was a lot beneath the surface of which I was mostly or totally unaware.

Why aren't we taught how to be in relationship with self? Most people tell me they were raised to believe that focus on self makes one "selfish," and that's not acceptable in social consciousness. Interesting. We've been taught to believe we don't really matter in our own lives. We don't count. Yet, when most people delve below the surface of their beingness and doingness at the time of their wake up call, they find they've spent their entire lives trying to show the world how much they do count!

First and foremost, waking up is about getting very clear on how you behave with *yourself*. You will look at things like: how well you accept yourself, care for yourself, and Love and trust yourself. You will also dig into how you deny yourself, berate yourself, and guilt, and punish yourself. Do you know whether you count in your own life? Can you see how a subconscious belief that you *don't* count could cause you to make everything in your life more about external factors than about you? I felt like I was not that important in my life. As a result, I focused externally for validation, caring, support, understanding, and more. Over time, I built up subconscious anger, resentment, and guilt related to those beliefs.

Check-In

Take a moment now to notice what is coming up for you in the area of "I don't matter enough in my own life." Are you recalling bad relationships, unfulfilling careers/jobs, physical fatigue, emotional trauma and stress, financial struggle, and/ or loss? I certainly did! Take a couple of deep breaths, and as you exhale, say, "This is great!" And believe me, it is. You can't change what you're unwilling to look at. You can't create a great life if you choose to stay asleep-at-the-wheel of the unfulfilling life you're already living.

Your relationship with you is the most important relationship in transformation to your **Living Happy To Be ME!** self. Why? Confucius said it like this…

Wherever you go, there you are.

I say it like this…

I can only be the Essence I express as me.

What we both mean is that everything you experience comes from inside of you, and wherever you go, what's inside you is right there with you. You can change your environment, leave friends, lose partners, jettison jobs. You can go on vacation to unwind. You can drown sorrows in alcohol, food, or other indulgences (and I did all of the above). But none of it will matter until you go to the heart of the matter—your heart and your feelings about and behaviors towards yourself.

The Truth of the matter is that you are meant to experience Abundance, Peace, Love, Freedom, and Joy in the outer world because this is who you really are on the inside. When you experience lack, struggle, fear, abandonment, disease, material loss, depression, or other "negative" experiences, you're being called into a realization that there's interference altering your vibration. It's embedded in your idea of who you are, and it's going to be with you wherever you take you. These undesirable situations are reflecting back to you what's going on inside you that you need to get a handle on and transform. Life's "bad" situations are the fertile ground into which you can sow seeds of higher awareness, and awaken to your Higher Consciousness. Your life is happening for you to get clear on who you're being to yourself.

When something detrimental is within your "you-ness," you can't escape it until you dismantle the false beliefs that anchored it there in the first place. Until you detach from the anchor and re-connect instead to inner Truth, your outer experience will be less than what you are fully capable of, or will be spent doing something other than what you are truly intended for.

What are the aspects of this inner relationship for you? What is your relationship with you based on? Are your choices driven by pleasing yourself or others? Do you act based on feelings of empowerment or feelings of fear? Do you believe in yourself or are you riddled with self-doubt? When the little judge inside you speaks, what does he or she say? What do you guilt yourself about? What do you shame yourself about? How are you telling yourself that you're inadequate or unworthy? What are the triggers? Are you even aware how often you're doing it? It's time to see if you're an asset to yourself or if you are your own Achilles heel.

Here's how to start seeing it: Listen to your mind chatter or mind dialog. What is the nature of that conversation? If you're an asset to you, your mind dialog says things that are enriching, expansive, nurturing, healthy, life-giving, peaceful, and HAPPY. You feel supported by yourself. You move through your life feeling solid and purposeful even when you don't know where the road is taking you. You feel like you have a perpetually full tank and feel optimistic in every situation. People experience your presence as uplifting and fun. You laugh easily and often, even at yourself. You are fulfilled in the midst of emptiness.

If you are your own Achilles heel, your mind tells you things like "Shame on you!" or "What were you thinking!?..." or "You're such an idiot!" or "I can't believe you can't figure this out!" or "You're such a loser!" or "You're too fat! (or skinny, ugly, pig-headed etc)." You feel alone most of the time, even when you're in a room full of people. You feel like people don't really "get" you, and you spend lots of time trying to be understood. Your tank often feels empty, but no amount of refilling with outer world fuel seems to make you feel full. Relationships are often dull, disconnected, and perhaps even disabling. You feel like your life is missing something essential,

> The Truth of the matter is that you are meant to experience Abundance, Peace, Love, Freedom, and Joy in the outer world...

and if you could only find it, all would be well. You notice patterns of taking one step forward and then two steps back.

Having a bad or no relationship with yourself, doesn't mean your life is in shambles. I was very successful, accomplished, financially well-off, etc. I was also disconnected, self-judging, chronically fatigued, lonely, and my own harshest critic. I pushed myself relentlessly to do more, so I could have more, and could feel happy and successful. In the long-run, it didn't work.

Check-in

Let's pause to do a little exercise that can help you get below the surface of your relationship with yourself. Let's start to see how you might be your Achilles heel or an asset. Close your eyes and take several deep breaths. Connect within in silence for a couple moments. Gradually allow your focus to shift to a time when you were doing something important. It could be baking a birthday cake for a loved one, writing a report for work or school, or packing something fragile or valuable. Be sure it was something you felt was very important at the time.

Now imagine that you did something "wrong" in the process, like dropped an egg on the floor, or lost the document, or broke the valuable item. What are the first three things you say to yourself/about yourself in your inner dialog? Write them down here.

Who am I to me?

My inner dialog:

_____

_____

_____

_____

_____

_____

_____

_____

_____

Now, take a couple moments and be with what you wrote. What does it feel like? Close your eyes again and imagine that you are saying these things to a young girl or boy standing in front of you. How do *they* respond? Do they throw their arms around you in a hug of safety, relief and delight? Or do they shrink, tear up, and cry? Does it feel like they're thankful, or are they hurt and dejected at what you just said?

Now, imagine that boy or girl is *you*. How do the words of your inner mind feel when you allow them to consciously land in your heart? Do *you* feel thankful or hurt and angry? If you feel even the slightest bit uncomfortable, sad, hurt, angry, resentful, or fearful because of this dialog, there is something to be healed in your relationship with yourself. You will probably also have to take a journey of discovery to find all the ways you learned how to treat yourself so badly.

If you are unwilling to go deeply into a journey of self- knowledge, you risk walking around like Pig-Pen, the Charles Shultz character popularized in the comic strip "Peanuts." You could be unknowingly dragging your emotional-junk-in-the-trunk around and unconsciously allowing it to spill into your outer world and get in the way of your ability to create what you truly desire.

I had no idea what about me was holding me back. My subconscious anger translated to aggressiveness and assertiveness (a.k.a. bullying) to make progress happen at work, within organizations or on teams. People felt fearful in my presence, and I thought that was working for me. Subconscious feelings inside me of being unlovable, unworthy, and inadequate translated to a driven nature, and pushing to get people to "see," hear, understand, and value me. Fear of loss, fear that I would never measure up, and fear that people were out to get me, kept me feeling like my life was always going to be about working hard and struggling, and ultimately, that I would never have what I really wanted. Little by little, this is what my outer world reflected. And remember, all this was going on under the surface as I was living what I rationalized was a wonderful life, and while I experienced some very positive outcomes!

If you are experiencing muck and yuck on the outside right now, the trouble is within.

The inner demons, as many people call them, can keep you running in circles wondering what is blocking you from having the kind of life you desire. But it doesn't have to be that way. That's why the **Wake Up!** Step is so critical. You must be brave and dive in. You must trust that it's better to be awake, dealing objectively and lovingly with what needs to change, than to be asleep-at-the-wheel of your life as those things victimize you. It is only with eyes wide open and heart clear that you can align with your **Magnificent Essence** and create the Heaven-on-Earth experience you are meant to have.

> Moment by moment the Holy Spirit will work with your beliefs, taking you step by step as you unwind your mind from the many false concepts that you believe keep you safe and make you happy. Only the release from these false beliefs can bring you true happiness and lasting peace. ~ David Hoffmeister

Your other option might be to ignore the call from your heart to do this exploration. You might decide that it feels like too much work, it might take too long, or you might get stuck in the muck and never surface again. Or your intellect might be having trouble with the less concrete, not at all black-and-white and less provable parts of my message.

Notice which part of you is suggesting these outcomes or raising these doubts. Notice that beneath them all is an idea that you having all of you is not important. Some aspect of you is saying that you having all of you could take too long or be a distraction from the goals at hand. Who within you would decide that you having the *Truth* of you is too much work?

The only aspect of you that would fear you waking up is the aspect of you that thrives when you are asleep—the ego. It's interesting that Dr. Wayne Dyer and others have made ego into an acronym meaning "Edging God Out." This is what is happening when the ego keeps us from pursuing a connection of meaning and fulfillment with our inner Divine Light. The ego is rooted in fear: fear of loss, fear of failure, fear of persecution, fear of its own demise. Ego is the very antithesis of Essence. The ego cannot run you when you are connected to your Essence. The more you can quiet its presence in your life, the more you can experience what you are really made of!

Answer the call. Respond to the nudges you're feeling within and experiencing in your outer world. Trust that there is more to you than you may be aware of and it's better and brighter. Go below the surface of you and look at the anchored, emotional wounds, and habitual, triggered responses and see what is real and what is a story from the false self. No matter where you are in a spiritual awakening, you can go higher into your Consciousness by going deeper into you.

Once you discover what's really been running you, you're at a choice point. You can choose to keep it or choose to create a **Shake Up!**

Step 2: Shake Up! And Release What is Not the True You

Those things we stuff, try so hard to ignore, they are the very things begging for release - the things that hold the promise of hope, the flame of freedom. ~ Jo Ann Fore

Another favorite Einstein quote of mine is, "Insanity is doing the same thing over and over and expecting a different result." In this Step you have the opportunity to assess how much of what you're doing in your life is this kind of insanity. Choosing to do a **Shake Up!** is choosing to make somewhat massive changes in you. The changes take place in how you express yourself, and through Universal Spiritual Laws that govern our existence, dissolve attachments to anything in your life that causes you to feel victimized. Shaking things up is choosing what stays and what goes.

Imagine you receive a box as you complete the **Wake Up!** Step, and on the outside, it says "This is me." Inside, there's a big deck of blank cards. You take the cards out and one-by-one on individual cards, you write your most prominent beliefs, values, habits, and stories from the past that you feel define you. You also capture any new realizations from your current awakenings. Then imagine throwing all the cards up in the air, and deciding with conscious intent to pick *some* of them up to create your new "This is ME" deck. Notice the old cards probably reflect more of the lower case m.e. These would be your ego-reflective expression and experiences of your life, most of which were created through misperception, faulty interpretation and ongoing negative conditioning. The later deck, should be very different, as it is born from applying the Steps in this process, and therefore, will reflect the more awakened, aligned, Conscious you that is the capital **M.E.** of **Magnificent Essence.**

The **Shake Up!** is the process of tossing the cards in the air. You choose to let go of everything that makes up the you that you *think* you are and start from scratch. As much as possible, you zero-base your ideas of yourself. You return to the innocence of a child and start from scratch. As the **Wake Up!** Step shines light on the ways the false-self has been driving your expression and your experiences of your life, the **Shake Up!** Step gives you a chance to make new choices. I call this taking a Soul Inventory. Knowing that you are Image and Likeness, knowing that you have Divine Purpose and Potential, knowing that you are a precious and perfect Divine Being, and always have been, you then look at whatever you have been doing and believing, and *not* doing and *not* believing, and decide what feels in alignment with the True You. Everything else has to go.

This is the time to claim what you want to keep as you move forward in your life and as you simultaneously commit to releasing the aspects of the false-self that you now *know* you don't need anymore. How do you know you don't need them? You have discovered how you created them, and you have reviewed how they are not working for you. Think of this as your opportunity to purify your relationship with yourself. You get rid of the toxic aspects that are holding you back and pulling you down, and you get lighter and your life gets easier. It's a lightening up from letting go!

In the beautiful book, *Help Thanks Wow—The Three Essential Prayers*, author Anne Lamott says:

> We learn through pain that some of the things we thought were castles turn out to be prisons, and we desperately want out. But even though we built them, we can't find the door.

A little inside clean-up can help you find the door. I know that every time I do even the smallest bit of sprucing up in one room, my whole house feels lighter and brighter, it smells good, and I feel great. The **Shake Up!** Step is the *inside-you* house cleaning that helps you have that same uplift. This is your time to lovingly do some house cleaning from the 'who am I being and

why?' perspective. A really good house cleaning happens when the cleaning crew doesn't just address the visible dirt; the stuff on the surface they can easily see.

A really good house cleaning happens when someone goes on a dirt *hunt*—when someone chooses to be in relentless pursuit of the hidden stuff. Are you willing to do that for yourself? Are you willing to relentlessly pursue getting clear on all you have been doing and believing, and *not* doing and *not* believing, that is part of what's keeping your life from being as shiny and bright as it can be? Will you stop at the obvious things, like eating too much sugar, or will you also go for the subtle culprits, like what's hiding underneath your decision to keep doing a job you hate or continuing in a relationship that is hurting you? Remember it's about what's going on deep inside of you—most likely at the subconscious and unconscious levels of your expression. It's not about what's outside you; the things outside of you are simply a reflection. You can't win if you focus there.

There is such inner power gained from doing the kind of inquiry that enables you to explore deeply enough to really shake things up. It starts with being a conscious observer of yourself, sort of like a fly on the wall. Your clues lie in the things you say and don't say, what you are willing to do and not willing to do, in what gets under your skin and ticks you off. Clues are also amidst the stories you tell yourself about others and those you tell about yourself, what makes you smile or cry, and why that something you do is 'so you.' Notice what feels like it fits the True You and what doesn't. Then ask yourself questions to get below the surface and understand *why* it feels like it fits or doesn't. Finally you make a choice to keep it as it is, keep it but alter it, or Bless and release it.

This Step was awesome for me! Once I could see the aspects of the false me, how my misperceptions, mixed up interpretations and coping behaviors had given birth to her, and how deeply I was attached to keeping her alive out of fear, I was more than happy to Bless and release her to claim the True ME.

Ask yourself, what kinds of anchors could be weighing you down? Do you suspect that you are caught in a web of guilt, shame, blame, or punishment? Can you feel hidden, age-old emotional junk-in-the-trunk clogging up your ability to discern your heart's call? Do you see signs that you have been telling yourself you're less-than, inadequate, unworthy, or unlovable? How? Are you ready to see the "not-you," so you can choose the True You? It's how you get more of the things you want and less of the things you don't.

Fear and guilt are your enemies. If you let go of fear, fear lets go of you. If you release guilt, guilt will release you. How do you do that? By choosing to. It's that simple.
~ Donald L. Hicks

Here are the places I hunted for my conscious, subconscious and unconscious self-expression that wasn't serving me. I found plenty to put in my personal "Lighten Up and Let Go" pile:

Sacred Cow Beliefs

Think of these as any phrase or idea that you have adopted as a "truth" in your life. I mentioned earlier about the beliefs I'd adopted from significant others and social consciousness in my early years: the feelings of inadequacy associated with being a Black female; the ideas about struggle and working hard to prove myself. There were also beliefs about money having to come from hard work, relationships being unfulfilling, and men being untrustworthy. There were the shame and guilt that organized religion had instilled in me; beliefs about what it meant to be a friend and how one demonstrated friendship, and so much more.

Most of these were simply by-products of what was going on around me—what I overheard and what I experienced being played out in my environment. I took it all personally and made it about me. No one sat me down and taught me those things, nor did I ever *consciously* decide they were true or *consciously* choose to build my idea of myself on them as a foundation. But nonetheless, the beliefs became rooted within, and they began to be dominant parts of my subconscious self-image over time.

They don't have to be negative or arise from abusive or victimizing experiences. "Beauty is in the eye of the beholder" certainly doesn't sound bad. But if you are the beholder, gazing at yourself in the mirror, and you have trouble finding the beauty, it can make you forever look outside yourself for validation. "Whatever is worth having is worth working hard for," sounds like sage advice about striving and achieving. Yet, at the same time, it is filled with lack and limitation, and subconsciously sets us up to look for the hardest paths to having anything we really want.

What beliefs will you uncover in your **Wake Up!** that are a part of the false-self, established long ago, by accident, that you can choose to heal and release?

Rules of Engagement

These are the little things that structure how you participate (or don't) in relationships and situations throughout your life. These rules governed when and how I spoke, how I dressed, when I made eye contact, who I called "friend," how I reacted to perceived wins and losses, when I rested, who I had sex with, what/when/how I should have or should not have done in relationships, what was acceptable for other people to do to/for me, etc. All the expectations I put on myself and on others were in this category. All the assumptions I had made about what I was hearing and seeing through my interactions were in this category.

What are these for you? A great place to look for these is in your knee-jerk reactions. Those are the responses you give to things that happen around you, and that are also so much a part of your 'way of being,' that you don't even realize you're doing them. What are those in-a-split-second actions that you take when someone says or does something that impacts you? They will tell you loads about your Rules of Engagement.

I often hear voices from childhood underneath my old Rules—my parents, the minister or Sunday school teacher, and my kindergarten or elementary school teachers. Their often strict do's and don'ts created assumptions about how the world works, and for a while, they may have been valid and they may have served me. But in all our lives, there comes a time to re-evaluate if the past ideas about things are the ideas we want running us now. So the *now* question for you is are your assumptions from the past that create Rules of Engagement still valid? Or can you see how they have nothing to do with what is real for you now? What are these Rules for you and how well are they serving your True Self in today's terms? Who are you *without* your past behavioral conditioning and the Rules of Engagement your old conditioning created? Is it time to get to know *this* you and experience your life as *this* person?

Anger and Resentment

It was hard for me to deal with this category because I didn't want to admit that I was an angry and resentful person underneath the surface, and most of the things I was angry and resentful about were way in the past. But as I allowed myself to feel the anger and explore the resentments, I was able to see how they contributed to my blind-spots, which I would hear about from friends, family, and colleagues. I also saw how they showed up as physical illnesses. By the time I was 30, I had manifested high blood pressure and in my 40's was diagnosed with a benign super arrhythmia

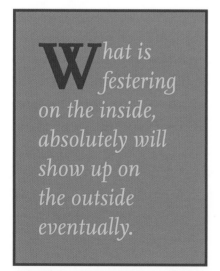

What is festering on the inside, absolutely will show up on the outside eventually.

—both heart conditions that I now attribute to stuck anger at myself and others, and fear of intimacy that had constricted my heart. The anger was not really just inside me. It showed up in my outer expression. People could see it on my face and feel it in my energy, even when I didn't know it was showing. Sometimes, it just blew out of me like an eruption from a volcano.

The negative emotional impact of childhood experiences, like playground embarrassments, being called names, not being picked for kickball teams, not getting into the high school sorority, having the boy I liked like someone else—or worse, like me in private but not in public, moving again, and again, and *again*. The things I took personally when people around me said things that hurt my feelings or did things that felt to me like abandonment. Resentments grew, as over time, the angers festered. It became about what people should have done to make amends, and how they should have known that they'd slighted me, and "if they really cared about me, they would have... [fill in the blank]." These ideas in me came from the Rules of Engagement and the Sacred Cow Beliefs that I established and followed to run my life.

Once you get clear on the way your attachments to anger and resentments are poisoning your expression and experience, you will want to let them go. Otherwise, you may manifest a real, live experience of the saying, "If you are holding onto anger and resentment, you are drinking the poison and waiting for the other person to die." It may show up as depression, cancer, or some other loud calling to shift your life. What is festering on the inside, absolutely will show up on the outside eventually.

Guilt and Shame

I think of guilt and shame as ongoing suffering over past experiences. It's sad to realize the amount of external guilt and shame that we are *taught* to take on. It comes from so many angles, including parents, friends, religion, and social consciousness. Somehow, we convince ourselves that it's right and appropriate to accept it, and then we carry it with us for the rest of our lives. We become experts at beating ourselves up over and over for the same thing. It's like an insidious termite eating us up from the inside. Specifically, guilt tends to be a psychological condition of inner conflict caused when we measure ourselves against some standard and conclude we are "less-than." For many people, it's an external standard like societal or religious morals, our parents' ambitions for us, our company's code of ethics, or social consciousness. But we often also add on top of that metric, a *separate* evaluation against our own Sacred Cow Beliefs and Rules of Engagement. This is how shame arises within.

Shame can leave an even deeper inner wound. Shame is born when, even though we measure up or even exceed the *external* standards against which we are measured, because of our *internal* values, we still judge ourselves as wanting. Thus the bully may feel powerful when his mates are cheering him on, but inside, there may be intense self-hatred building as he violates his own inner compass about how he should or should not be treating other people.

For me, guilt and shame included all the ways I judged myself as letting myself or others down. When I missed a penalty kick, or got in trouble at school and "embarrassed" my parents/family, or didn't get an "A" on a test when I believed I should have, or just because my hair was kinky and saw myself as less pretty than the girls whose hair was straight.

Sometimes, we turn subconscious anger or resentment into a reason to feel guilty or shameful, and that haunts us too. I was talking with a beautiful, smart, accomplished woman who was having trouble with her relationship with money. She worked hard, stayed positive, said affirmations and intentions, and actually made a great living most of the time. But she still often felt like something was in the way of her making the big money she desired. There was too much struggle and sometimes heartache along the way. What she found through deep exploration was that her first connection to "earning" money came through something she was ashamed of...bed wetting. She recalled that, as a little girl, her parents had paid her a nickel every time she made it through the night without wetting the bed. This anchored an emotional connection between receiving money and a feeling of shame, and of having to prove her worthiness. It followed her into adulthood without her even knowing it.

Over time, you can get so turned around and stuck in subconscious thoughts of not measuring up that you don't notice how convoluted it's all becoming. Sadly, you can be inaccurate in the judgments on which the guilt and shame are based. The Sacred Cows and Rules of Engagement you are living by may be so skewed in one direction or another, that you continually feel like you don't measure up. The exploration to get below the surface and engage each one is critical to the lightening up and letting go process of **Living Happy to Be ME!**

> ## You will actually be freeing yourself from what *never* should have been planted in your idea of yourself in the first place!

It's time to lay down the burden of carrying these inaccurate judgments and the diminishment of living that is fueled by them. It's time to claim higher ground and have the life you were meant to live. It's time to have *you*.

Fears and Victimology

> So many of us live our lives in fear
> disguised as practicality. ~ Jim Carrey

All emotional fear is from thoughts and beliefs. Some of the fears within us, like those hiding beneath the Sacred Cow Beliefs and Rules of Engagement, are by-products of things that happened around us, as well as to us. Have you ever met anyone who was terrified of dogs although they never had a bad experience with a dog? Where did that fear come from? Have you ever felt fear about something and didn't know why? That's the kind of below-the-surface emotional block I'm talking about here. The dance with the **Shake Up!** Step is designed to address fear instilled in the emotional self. Fear that is a remnant of traumatic experiences may be psychological as well as emotional, and may require different approaches to augment what I teach in this book.

> The definition of Karma is the disappointments of
> the ancestors visited on the children.
> ~ Swamiji Chetanananda

This quote reminds me that some of the victimology that I was attached to in the past wasn't even mine. Some of it came from ancestral history that was being played out/handed down through generations of storytelling about the situations, and the fears, anger and resentments they caused. It continues to land on each subsequent generation, and some landed on me. The beliefs I created from my family's history are mine, but they started with actual experiences in other people, elsewhere.

Emotional fears come from the stories we tell ourselves about the various experiences in our lives. Over time, they establish a fear pattern. And believe it or not, these fears could have been established when we weren't even able to use words to describe what we were feeling. As you read in my story, I know that my mother was in fear and dread when she was carrying me. While it had nothing to do with me, I believe that experiencing her sensations of fear created my fear-based relationship with the world before I even entered it. I've heard the stories of how much I cried as a baby: "Whether you were wet or dry, hungry or fed, tired or not, there was a period during which you would not stop crying." My Mom told me of how she went to the pediatrician on the military base where we lived at the time, and asked him to give me something to give her some peace. The doctor replied, "I don't drug my babies."

Victimology, a sense that we've been emotionally hurt by something someone else has done or said, can be instilled the same way. We can be victimized by how

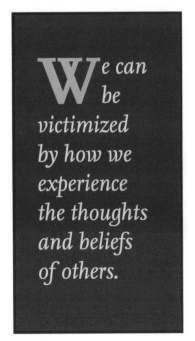

We can be victimized by how we experience the thoughts and beliefs of others.

we experience the thoughts and beliefs of others. The mother who passes down her experiences through story-telling and cautionary prohibitions meant to protect her child can create a fear-based mentality within the child without even knowing it's happening. A story about "the way things are" in life can create a fear-based reluctance to experiencing that situation at all. As a result, there's no opportunity to have the situation happen, and therefore no opportunity to disprove the belief.

An example of this is the connections I made to some of the stories I heard as a child of what it meant to be Black. I recall feelings of nervous tension inside whenever I entered a room, walked down the street, or wanted to join a group. It was a fear of being judged because of the color of my skin.

It came with a dread that all the eyes looking at me would see difference and judge it as "less than." Before any words were spoken or behaviors towards me displayed, I had already braced myself for what I had been conditioned to believe was inevitable. The stories that I heard and reframed in my own mind, created an experience of being victimized before anything had actually occurred.

Simultaneously, I would create a series of actions to protect myself from the judgments I assumed were already present. I would carefully choose my words (the bigger the better) to sound as articulate and smart as possible, I might make myself the brunt of a joke or laugh at others' jokes even when I didn't think they were funny, and I would be very careful about what I let people see or experience of me.

These and other self-abandoning behaviors were part of what I thought I needed to do to be accepted and liked.

Can you see the downward spiral? First, my subconscious idea of not being lovable created the idea of being a victim. Second, fear of being victimized by their reactions to me resulted in my withholding aspects of myself to avoid a negative experience. Instead, I engaged with a somewhat false self, sharing only what I thought would make me the most likeable. Over time, catching myself wearing masks and hiding created shame and guilt because I didn't like feeling like I had to do it, but I was too afraid not to. That level of fear resulted in even more fear of sharing the real me. The energy of fear and victimology caused deeper and deeper withholdings as part of escape and avoidance, and the energy and beauty and value of the True Valerie got buried with it.

Fear gets created, behaviors to escape or avoid feeling the fear come next, and in the end, we may become victims of our own behaviors as a result of the downward spiral, rather than from what we feared in the first place! It's important to be conscious of where fear comes from in our lives, and of our conditioned patterns of feeling or avoiding feeling it. Our fear of loss, whether it be loss of face, loss of money, loss of standing, loss of stuff, can actually result in loss of the True Self and the love that we are here to give and receive.

Victimology can also result because someone really does create the opportunity for us to perceive we've been victimized. Let's say that my worst fear in the story above actually happens and one of the people I encounter says or does something intended to make me feel bad. Maybe they call me a name, close the door in my face, or in some other way make it clear they don't accept or like me. They're not really making a statement about me. What's really happening is they're showing who *they* are. They are letting me see what's going on inside of them. They're displaying their Sacred Cow Beliefs, their Rules of Engagement, their Burning Angers and Resentments, and their Fears and Victimology. My presence was simply the trigger for their expression of what's going on inside of them.

> ## Reject your sense of injury and the injury itself disappears. ~ Marcus Aurelius

The reality is that I don't have to feel like a victim because of the way someone else expresses their inner false self. If I can experience them being them, without taking it personally, I don't have to feel hurt. But when I take *their* stuff on as though it's really about me, ultimately I lose, because it tends to create a new association with being victimized, and a deepening cycle of fear, anger and resentment that is self-perpetuating and self-fulfilling.

Think of how many times in a day you have the opportunity to react to what people say and do, as if it's true about you. Imagine how these would get stacked up in your mind over the course of your life. On top of them, stack all the times you changed your behavior to try to make them see you differently and value you more. You'd be living your life to get them to see you or value you a certain way, meanwhile, morphing yourself so much that you can get completely off track with being you and getting what you really want. This is how you can end up asking, "How did I get here?" and being sad that your life *is* your life. It doesn't have to be this way.

Past Memories of Happy Times and Anticipation of the Future

This is often the toughest category for many people to understand. They ask why I would say they need to get rid of happy memories if they feel better when they recall them. My answer is that it depends on how they're engaging those memories. Casual moments spent reliving the past are fine. It can be beneficial to revisit times gone by here and there, especially when you're wanting to understand them better and see what gift for you was hidden underneath the surface experience. However, spending too much time living from the past means you are not experiencing fully the life you have today. The same is true of constantly making today about the future.

Sometimes, when life today doesn't feel good, you may resort to escape/ avoidance of the here and now so you don't have to feel what the situational dynamics of the here and now are bringing up. For example, if the here and now has job loss, bankruptcy, and a chronic illness in it, you might feel an emotional urge to disconnect so you don't have to feel what you associate with job loss, bankruptcy and chronic illness. Perhaps the feelings are about being inadequate, inept, stupid or a failure. So you block those feelings out and tell yourself of great times gone by or focus on how great it will be at some point in the future.

But since your life is happening only in the now, you're missing it. You could be blocking the very happiness, success and fulfillment you want to experience because the energy you need to create it, isn't present in the here and now.

I once mentored a 50-something woman who was frequently talking about her past. She only related to her life through stories about situations and relationships that represented an entire way of life that she loved, but that was no longer. She judged her present situation as far less happy than the stories she recalled from her past. As a result, she characterized herself as unhappy. But here's the interesting thing... she had a great life in the present...she just couldn't see it.

> To experience the fullness of your life in the present, you must keep your focus in the present.

She had a lovely apartment near the ocean, lots of friends who adored her and wanted to share time with her, enough money for her needs and wants, good physical and mental health and more. But because she was evaluating it using a yardstick that was totally based in the past, and the present didn't provide as much excitement as she'd experienced in the past, in the present, she could only feel loss, lack and limitation.

In looking back at my own life as I did the dance of the **Shake Up!** Step, I was surprised to find how much time I spent in the future. I was making choices for what to do in the present predominantly so I could have a particular result in the future, without paying attention to what those choices meant for my here and now. One example is working myself ragged so I could ensure a promotion at some point, not fully realizing how much I was sacrificing to that plan in the here and now.

You simply cannot have it both ways. To experience the fullness of your life in the present, you must keep your focus in the present. This means visiting the past and future briefly, noticing what the triggers are that cause you to do so, and then returning your focus back to what serves you best—the here and now.

The **Shake Up!** Step gives you the opportunity to stop the madness that may be underneath your actions—even the ones that look good from a surface-only view. I am not saying that all fear is bad or that you can't be angry. The key here is how are you engaging in the fear? Are you feeling it and flowing it or are you becoming it? Are you able to feel and express your feelings of anger, or are you an angry person because past anger is still stuck inside and showing up in all your relationships? Are your values and beliefs really ones you want to keep because you value and believe them, or are they left-overs from what you learned from your parents or teachers or ministers? How do these aspects of your life underlay the way you live your life?

A life lived from the influence of negative conditioned patterns of behavior from the past is not a life fully lived. There are probably very few people on the planet who are free from having some combination of Sacred Cow Beliefs, Rules of Engagement, Burning Angers and Resentments, Fears and Victimology, and Past/Future focus running them. Depending on how aware you are of their existence and how attached you are to their presence, you may have limited ability to feel your true here and now emotions, and to share your hearts fully, even with yourself.

The goal of the **Shake Up!** is to *create space for expansion in your life from the inside out.* By releasing things that block your connection to and alignment with yourself as a Divine Being, you free yourself into a more True expression of you. You want to free yourself from anything from the past that could be shackling off your heart, imprisoning your ability to be authentically Happy. For most of you, the answer lies in the categories above. The late Dr. Norman Vincent Peale, an American Protestant minister considered by many to be the grandfather of the positive psychology movement said:

> There is a spiritual giant within you, which is always struggling to burst its way out of the prison you have made for it.

You have a golden opportunity right now to unshackle the spiritual giant within you. Jump into the **Shake Up!** Step and relentlessly pursue your freedom. Go below the surface of everything you *think* you hold dear—beliefs, values, habits, and relationships. Jettison the junk-in-your-emotional-trunk. Free your Divine Self from what is holding you back.

I can't manifest the new, when I'm mired in my old muck and goo.

The playfulness of this quote comes from my love of Dr. Seuss and his amazing imagination. I think of creativity and imagination as foundations for an authentically happy experience, and as I've released old things that weren't serving me anymore—the muck and goo beneath the surface of my expression of me—my expression has become more playful and creative. The playful (sometimes quite silly), creative aspects of me are expressions from the reservoir of happiness within.

You have this same reservoir within you. As you re-evaluate your attachments to people, expectations, standards, entitlement, and rules, you give yourself the opportunity to tap into it. As you free yourself of old angers, resentments, judgments, and punishments that you're pointing inside and outside of you, you allow its call to be felt within. But don't stop there.

There's one more category worth mentioning, and that's your "stuffology," what author and medical intuitive Caroline Myss calls material possessions. Stuffology can block your flow as much as emotional baggage. Why would universal love send more to a house or heart that can't give love to what it already has? Again, this is not about living an austere life because you're opening up to the Divine Nature of you. It's about being clear on what having the stuff *represents* in your idea of who you are, and whether it's related to the false self or the True you.

I have chosen to do some major downsizing of stuffology over the past decade. I had accumulated a lot along my journey. Boxes of photos I never looked at; dozens of mugs, t-shirts, refrigerator magnets, and other tchotchkes from my various travels; more than 50 pairs of shoes, many of which matched only one outfit; books I wouldn't read again, love letters, jewelry, empty bottles of wine I'd made "keepsakes" because they marked a special point in time, and the list went on. It seems like the cycle of having stuff ends up being: the more stuff you have, the more stuff you need, and the more your stuff needs from you in return.

Believe it or not, your stuff is pretty needy! Your stuff needs a place to stay, so if you have a lot, you need a lot of space. A bigger house needs someone to clean it. The lawn around the big house needs someone to tend it. The once-a-year stuff like skis and snorkel gear need a place to be stored for the rest of the year. Major housing decisions about square footage are made every day based on keeping and storing stuff. I remember one of my realizations during the **Shake Up!** Step being that I didn't own my stuff…my stuff *actually owned me*!

As my journey to lighten up and let go in my life deepened, I found the will to release a lot. Some was by necessity: when I could no longer pay my corporate executive's mortgage on my new entrepreneur's income, the house had to be released. When the smaller house came in, lots of the stuff that would have to fit somewhere in that house had to go. It wasn't easy while I was in the energy of the false self, filled with lack and limitation ideas. The stuffology was part of my identity. It made me feel special, liked, seen, valued. It gave me a way to measure myself against what was outside of me. It gave me something to talk about that wasn't too intimate. It helped me feel pride in myself that I didn't always feel on a deeper, more genuine level.

But once I got connected to Truth, it was easy and simple! I no longer need the *things* in my life to be how I define myself or assess my value in the world. I am connected to and affirm my value in the absolute—exactly as I am, just *because* I am— no stuff required! So while I may still have some really great stuff, my relationship with it is completely different. Talk about freedom!

Your **Shake Up!** has to be this pervasive. You are wanting to get to the place where you can see who you are without your old patterns of negative conditioned behaviors. You must allow it to touch every aspect of your life in order for it to serve you best. Know that as you create a vacuum in your life by releasing what no longer fits, you simultaneously create open space to receive what *really* is for you.

I love this little story in *Help, Thanks, Wow* about a nun who had begged God for years to take her character defects away from her. The nun tells how finally one day, God got back to her saying "I'm not going to take anything away from you, you have to give it to me." You are the master of your life. By shaking up the things that have guided how you have lived that life, you can create the life you've always dreamed of. There are no limits to what you can experience when you're free from things that block your connection to and alignment with your Essence. But you have to do it. You have to freely choose to give up what isn't working and pick a new option. This is how to claim your ongoing **Living Happy To Be ME!** Lightstyle. This is how you evolve into your Higher Consciousness.

Check-in

Let's pause for a moment and capture some things from your false-self that you are now willing to release. Is it defensiveness at questions, or hoarding for fear of not having enough? Is it working all the time or ignoring your inner voice? Is it that "friend" who always puts you down, or a fear of speaking from your heart? Capture and commit to at least three things you are willing to release.

What am I ready to let go of right here and now?

_____

_____

_____

_____

_____

_____

_____

_____

_____

_____

_____

_____

Now feel inside and see if you can hear any ideas coming up about what might happen once the things on your list are really no longer a part of you. Capture them here:

_____

_____

_____

_____

_____

_____

_____

_____

_____

_____

The Release

Now let's explore the release, and a couple of my favorite supportive rituals. Release can be as simple as saying "I'm done with this now," like the people who quit smoking cold-turkey. They hit a place where they say inside, this is over, and they have every other aspect of their being fall into lock-step with this choice. They make the choice one time, and it's done. Or is it?

I believe that what looks to an outsider like "sticking to it" after one single decision, is actually hundreds and thousands of subsequent in-the-moment choices that keep supporting the original choice. The difference between the smoker who quits cold-turkey and one who quits then relapses then quits and relapses, is that at some point during the process of "sticking to it," the person who relapses makes a *different* choice. They may *want* to maintain the abstinence, but at the actual choice-point, they choose, consciously or not, to light a cigarette, and they are back to being a smoker.

Have you ever been adamant that you were going to start or stop doing something, you kept up with it for a few days, a few weeks, or a couple months, and all of a sudden you were back to business as usual? Yes, I have been there too. I bless those situations that come to mind for me because it was becoming of aware of them that helped me get where I am today! Instead of being in inner guilt, shame or sadness about failing myself (with the inner voice saying "again!"), I know now that there was something out of alignment in the conscious and subconscious levels of the choices I was trying to live up to.

What I mean by that is while I may have *consciously* decided I wanted to eat more healthy for example (a form of self–love on the physical, emotional, psychological and spiritual levels), something below the surface in my subconscious was thwarting me (it's difficult to love yourself through conscious acts when your subconscious belief is that you are not very lovable). So I'd eat healthy to a point, and then poor eating habits would creep back in. A cycle would ensue, that included beating myself up a little each time I failed for not being more successful at giving myself the healthier and prettier figure I wanted. I couldn't figure out why it was so hard for me to persevere. At one point in my life, I was close to 190 pounds!

As I have released the subconscious thoughts about myself, who and what I am in the world, what I deserve to experience and have, and why, my ability to keep choosing over and over in my favor has soared. I also have a more realistic and aligned perspective about what's really important to/for me and why. I still eat French fries, pizza and ice cream (I don't see myself ever giving up Graeter's Black Raspberry Chip ice cream), but not for the reasons I used to, and not as frequently as I used to.

> **R**elease can be as simple as saying "I'm done with this now..."

The important point in this is: in all things, even your dance with the **4 Steps**, choice is an over-and-over-and-over-and-over gift. Each choice-point—the crossroads at which you find yourself hundreds of times every single day—is an opportunity for your Divine Soul Being Self to express, or for some aspect of your false self to express. You can either spiral up or spiral down. If you want to truly spiral up, then you must choose to release the internal thoughts and beliefs rooted in the false self. They don't serve you, except to show you where you have disconnected from Truth.

Saint Paul wrote, "... be ye transformed by the renewing of your mind" (Rom 12: 2). That's what the **Shake Up!** is designed to help you do. Refresh, renew, re-energize, your mind's-eye-view of you. It will be easier for you to make choices that reflect a renewal of the self-loving Essence of you, as you release the self-destructive, self-denying aspects of the false self.

Ceremonies, rituals, and rites of passage are and have been a part of life throughout the history of time. They are present in subtle and prominent ways in social, religious and political processes. Ceremony puts a punctuation mark around a particularly solemn, joyous, or important occasion, preserving the result and in some cases, tending to protect it from doubt and opposition. I love ceremony and ritual for all these reasons. I know it's no mystery that I love creating sacred space and marking special moments for myself and others—I'm bringing the punctuation mark to preserve the meaning and benefits of the moment forever.

The practices and rituals I share as part of the release process are meant to make it easier for you to go deeper and to consciously let go of what is no longer serving you. I go over the essential elements in this chapter, and you'll also have opportunities to put them into practice with the action steps later in the book.

Detachment

Attachment has to do with your relationship to things. You attach to things when you identify with them to the level of feeling they are a part of you or they exemplify who you want to be. In the book *Purifying the Heart*, by John Goldthwait, we read that there are two kinds of attachment: personal identification with thoughts and situations, and resisting thoughts and situations. In both circumstances the idea is that you are attached to *having* a belief or to *not* having it. In the former, you spend energy holding onto the belief, proving to yourself and others that the belief is real and true, worthy of your energy. Conversely, attachment can have you giving lots of energy to denying a belief, trying to prove to yourself and others that it is not real or true, or worthy of your energy. Have you ever found yourself arguing your point of view in a conversation, and suddenly, feeling a little discomfort with how fervently you're holding onto your perspective? That discomfort is your inner self trying to call your attention to your attachment and what it's doing to you and your relationship in that moment.

> Detachment is not that you should own nothing. But that nothing should own you. ~ Mali Ibn Abi Talib

Attachments to people, situations, things, and experiences can also keep you in the past and away from the good that is awaiting you in the present moment. Attachment happens when you indulge in thoughts and beliefs about yourself relative to people, situations, things, and experiences such that you identify your idea of *you* as being tied up with *them*. You decide you would be better off with or without them, and you cannot see an alternative to those thoughts and beliefs. So you set your life up to keep having them or to keep trying *not* to have them.

How do you know if you're identified with thoughts and beliefs? According to Goldthwait, "You are identified with thoughts if you entertain them, get absorbed in them, believe them, react emotionally to them, defend them, or act on them." In short, if they drive your emotional experiences, your personality or identity, you are personally entangled with them.

The way to release yourself from attachments is to practice detachment, or non-attachment, which is holding the posture of "disengaged observer." It means that whether good or bad, the situations in your life don't hook you or trigger you to "react" to them. You can experience them without judgment, and without trying to hang onto them or resist them emotionally. You don't entertain them, or become intrigued by them. You simply allow them to be as they are.

Deepak Chopra, spiritual teacher and author of the "The Seven Spiritual Laws of Success" provides this perspective on detachment:

> *In detachment lies the wisdom of uncertainty … in the wisdom of uncertainty lies the freedom from our past, from the known, which is the prison of past conditioning. And in our willingness to step into the unknown, the field of all possibilities, we surrender ourselves to the creative mind that orchestrates the dance of the universe.*

Being detached isn't about being disinterested or oblivious to what is going on around you. You still function in and participate with the goings on in your life. But you *respond* with present moment awareness of and alignment with the Higher Consciousness that you are, meaning you are an expression of your Essence of Love and Peace.

I love mantras or affirmations to help me practice principles for vibrant living, so I created some for the detachment principle. Try one or more of these and get into the embodied expression of them as you practice being the embodied expression of detachment in your life:

- I surrender to the flow of my life.

- I allow others to express themselves freely, and have their own experiences within their lives.

- I need do nothing; I need control nothing and no one.

- I release the need to judge things as right/wrong, good/bad, and allow everything to be as it is.

- I trust Divine Love and Wisdom are at work in everything I experience, and I am safe.

- I express myself freely without the need for approval from others.

- I let go of the past and I open my heart and mind to new experiences.

Forgiveness

I love talking about forgiveness. I see it as a powerful practice that can begin at any moment in time and has no end. Like a lot of what I teach in the book, and what I find true in all of Truth, forgiveness is elegant in its simplicity, yet awesomely powerful in its depth and pervasiveness. It's a topic that can easily expand to volumes, so for our purposes here, I'm keeping it focused on helping you understand and embrace it relative to the **Shake Up!** Step, and not an all-encompassing discussion.

I never did so well with the old-school 'forgive and forget' that I was taught as a child. I don't know about you, but the forgetting part was pretty tough! I rarely met people who were without stories about some transgression from the past that was eating them up inside. I would marvel at how the emotional energy present while retelling the story was almost as strong as the energy I imagined was present when the original offense occurred. I'm sure people would say the same thing about feeling my energy when I was in story-telling mode.

Forgiveness at its most basic level is about releasing your negative feelings toward a person or group who you believe has caused harm to you or others. Forgiving is not dependent on any other thing happening. That's it, plain and simple. It is not dependent on feeling that justice has been delivered. The other person doesn't have to agree with you that their transgression was wrong, and they don't need to feel remorse or apologize for you to forgive. In fact, they don't even need to know you're forgiving them. You just forgive.

Where some people have trouble with forgiveness is that they believe it means they let people off the hook for their actions. They believe it makes the forgiver do all the work, while the "perpetrator" does nothing. They feel it makes them look stupid, or keeps them vulnerable, or doesn't hold the other person accountable for their actions.

I don't agree with those perspectives. To forgive does not mean to condone or be blind to bad behavior. It doesn't mean that you don't hold people legally accountable for their actions, and it doesn't mean that you have to end up with positive feelings about them either. As a forgiving person, you can still let others know how their actions have hurt you. As a forgiving person, you can ask that others make amends. The idea is to do both in the energy of love that forgiveness represents.

Ultimately though, forgiveness isn't about the other person at all. Forgiveness is really about *you*. Forgiveness is how you bring peace back into *your* heart. Forgiveness is how *you* detach from anger, resentment, guilt, shame, blame, vengeance and any other heart-closing, psychologically and physiologically disruptive feelings towards the offender. Forgiveness is how you enable yourself to *flow* the feelings of pain associated with the situation, without *becoming* that pain. Forgiveness is what allows you to truly move on in your life, allowing the wounds to heal. Forgiveness is how the past stays in the past, rather than being played out again and again through similar situations with different perpetrators. In other words, the situation doesn't become a part of your identity or your destiny.

In general, studies show that the more forgiving one is, the more compassionate, agreeable, empathetic and trusting they are as well. Conversely, those who have trouble forgiving tend to be more difficult to deal with, needing to control situations and push for specific outcomes.

Here are some behavioral indicators that you are *not* in forgiveness:

- You continue to tell the story of the transgression, and your emotional energy is as powerful each time as it was when the transgression first happened.
- You hear yourself plotting a way to make him/her/them pay.
- You secretly wish something bad would happen as their cosmic payback.
- You avoid him/her/them so you don't have to be reminded of the wrong committed against you.
- You withdraw from or avoid them altogether.

Here are some behavioral indicators that you *are* in forgiveness:

- You hear yourself sending him/her/them prayers of healing.
- You feel compassionate toward him/her/them even while you feel the wrong committed against you.
- You feel peaceful inside when thinking about the transgression or when encountering him/her/them.
- You trust the situation happened to teach you something about yourself.
- You feel gratitude for what you learned/healed as a result of going through the situation.

Dr. Everett ("Ev") Worthington, Professor of Psychology at Virginia Commonwealth University, author and expert on forgiveness, uses what is called the two-chairs technique to help people release grievances. The perceived victim sits in Chair A and addresses the real, though not present, perpetrator symbolized by empty Chair B. The victim shares exactly how he/she feels about the situation. The victim then moves to Chair B and responds to the feelings as the offender might.

Sitting in the offender's place to explain why they acted as they did, the victim is asked to think outside their hurts and blame by putting themselves in the other's place. This helps them potentially see dynamics and circumstances within the situation that they had previously overlooked. This can open the way for seeing both sides of the story, which can lead to compassion and eventually forgiveness. At a bare minimum, the victim gets a chance to speak their wounds out loud to the person as if they were there, and with as much emotional intensity as is necessary, which can help free them from the feeling of suffering in silence. I have personally experienced a slight variation on this technique first-hand, and I embraced its ability to get the pain and blame outside of me, which created a sense of freedom as a result of the emotional release.

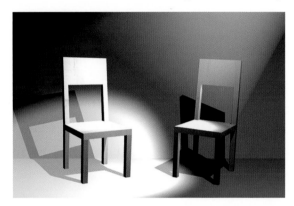

By far, my favorite forgiveness practice is the ancient Hawaiian/Polynesian prayer of reconciliation and forgiveness called ho'oponopono (pronounced ho-opono-pono). According to the Hawaiian dictionary, the word is translated as "to" (ho) "put to rights, to put in order, correct, amend" (ponopono). In its most simple explanation, the foundational principle of the practice is that the world we experience is our own creation. How we experience the world at any given moment is a product of our past experiences and our perspective, and as such we have responsibility for it. Based on that and other spiritual principles like the Law of Karma, to heal whatever we experience in the external world, we must take responsibility for it and heal ourselves on the inside. Proponents of the practice point out that taking responsibility isn't the same as saying it's your fault. It simply means you will do what is necessary to right whatever you perceive as wrong. In the case of ho'oponopono, 'whatever is necessary' is a simple but powerful 4-stanza prayer.

This prayer and the process in which it's used were perhaps made famous in the book *Zero Limits: The Secret Hawaiian System for Wealth, Health, Peace, and More* co-authored by Drs. Joe Vitale and Hew Len. Dr. Len first studied ho'oponopono under the late Hawaiian healer/priest Morrnah Nalamaku Simonea. Dr. Len is reported to have healed an entire ward for the criminally insane in the Hawaii State Mental Hospital, simply by using this process. The kicker is he never actually met with the patients at all. He sat in his office reading their files and engaging in the inside-out healing process of ho'oponopono. After four years, the hospital's criminally insane patient population had become so low, they closed the ward and the few remaining prisoners were transferred elsewhere.

Here's how I use and teach the process today:

1. Get into a quiet mental state, breathing deeply and rhythmically.
2. Call into your mind and heart a situation that needs healing.
3. Within yourself, feel the pain or trauma of the situation, and also allow yourself to feel compassion and empathy for the "transgressor/s."
4. With the energy of Love, address the Divinity within you saying: "I'm sorry. Please forgive me. Thank you. I love you." (The prayer is also taught as: "I love you. I'm sorry. Please forgive me. Thank you.")

I do this process when I'm concerned about:

*   Emotional states within me (guilt, shame, blame, fear, resentment, anger, loss).
*   Disturbances in the outer world (economic crises, human-on-human transgressions, hunger, natural disasters, harming the planet, etc.).
*   Feeling like someone has harmed me.
*   Feeling like I've harmed someone else.
*   Feeling like I've harmed myself.
*   Trouble in my relationships, my business, or my neighborhood.

Ho'oponopono is simple, elegant, and powerful. However as Dr. Len says himself, this is not a quick fix. The process is ongoing, and requires commitment and trust. The commitment is to healing yourself; the trust is that your own healing changes the world. The end result is what Dr. Len refers to as the state of Zero Limits—being totally free from the past, and fully aligned with your Divine Wisdom and Unconditional Love.

The Burning Bowl Ceremony

Another release ritual I like to practice, especially at the New Year, is the Burning Bowl Ceremony, which is also known as the Phoenix Ceremony. It's one of a number of popular "rites of renewal" performed in many New Thought churches, especially in the United States. A Burning Bowl Ceremony is a ritual to release negativity and ask for a positive replacement. You use it to release old patterns, beliefs, emotions or experiences, or anything that impedes you from realizing your True self. By releasing the old unwanted conditions, you clear the way for beginnings.

Again, I recommend it because it's simple yet powerful. Here are the steps:

1. Write the negative conditions that you would like to release from your life on a piece of paper. This turns the thoughts or feelings into something concrete outside of you.

2. Burn the paper in the bowl. This is believed to turn the concrete representation of the negative condition into smoke that is sent wafting to the Divine. Watch the paper burn completely, and as you do so, feel any inner remnants of the ideas on the paper burn off within you. Imagine them turning to ash and feel the sense of release from them no long being strong enough to hold you.

3. As you depart the ceremony, say to yourself words such as, "I am free, I am unlimited, there are no chains that bind me," or "I now move on, the past is gone forever," or (in the case of forgiveness) "I fully and freely forgive X (mentioning the name of the person); I loose him and let him go; He is free now, and I am free too."

4. Focus your attention on what you would like to create in your life as a new or "replacement" state. Write those intentions on paper, and meditate on them as a way to intentionally pray to the Divine for their manifestation.

I like to add my own variation to step 4 to keep it light and fun. So I love doing this as part of a larger celebration, for example, a full moon drumming circle or a beach barbecue. I take a few minutes of quiet time to capture my thoughts, burn the paper in the bonfire, and get on with the fun in the present moment. That includes drumming, dancing, chanting, walking the beach in search of heart rocks, and of course, roasting marshmallows! The idea here is that there's no need for release work to be a heavy or solemn experience. You don't have to wait until you're over-burdened by a list of negative situations. You can create it in a way that supports you—from the timing, to the frequency, to the variables.

Water Ceremony

I also like using water as part of the symbology of release. Water is a basic aspect of all life on earth, being central to existence since the dawn of time; water can also take life away. Water has been used in ritual, ceremony and religious practice all over the world throughout history. Some cultures attach religious significance to specific bodies of water. Waterfalls are sacred in the Japanese indigenous religion of Shinto; rivers are especially sacred in Hinduism, the River Ganges being most notable. In general, water is symbolic of cleansing and purification, as in releasing one from sin and suffering, and in preparation for connection with the Divine, either in prayer or through religious duties. Think of baptism in Christianity, Holy water in lavers in Catholic churches, and ritual cleansing before prayer in Islam and Judaism.

I have always loved being in connection with large bodies of water and I feel their cleansing effects deep within, on mental and emotional levels. I come away from time spent lounging by a lake or walking along the seashore feeling refreshed and renewed, as though the very nature of my being has been released from weight it no longer needed just by being there. I tend to vacation where I can get to water, and I dream of living waterfront one day. In the meantime, my Southern California beach community living is the next best thing!

I have done release rituals at the beach, but my favorite water ritual involves my bathtub and a ceremonial drowning, where immersion provides a more total from of cleansing and release. This ritual begins with a quiet meditation asking the inner self to reveal what blocks I am ready to release. Once I have the answers clear in my heart, I write them down on a piece of paper. While my bathtub is filling with water, I light candles and drum for a few minutes. Then I set my intention to release what I wrote from all aspects of my beingness. Once in the tub, I hold the piece of paper with my list on it, under the water while reciting this in my mind:

> *I hereby release myself from any and all aspects of these blocks. From this day forward, there is no significance to them and they hold no power over me. I hold the power of life over them, and I now take it away. They are drowned, and dead in me forever more. Thank you.*

I cleanse myself in the bath water for just 5 minutes, and then get out and wrap myself in my towel. I drum a little more in the peaceful acknowledgement that I have the power to choose what impacts my life as I watch the water run down the drain. I allow the energy of the things on the list to recede from my awareness as all the water recedes from the tub, and I center myself on the new freedom I just created.

Bubble Meditation

One last detailed idea I'd like to share here involves one of my favorite childhood playthings—soap bubbles. I have had a fascination with and love for bubbles as long as I can remember. I still carry them with me as an adult to bring more playfulness into situations and events! I've even carried the soapy bubble-making substance in a beautiful sterling vessel that could hang on a leather lanyard around my neck. Bubbles make me smile and laugh; I wonder at their symmetry, their iridescence, and I love watching how far they will float, sometimes connected to another bubble!

Believe it or not, there is potential spiritual significance in soap bubbles. Some say the significance lies in the wonder on the faces of those experiencing them. This sense of fascination at what appears on the surface to be a little inexplicable, relates to the mystical nature of life, our connection to one another and The Divine. Others talk about bubbles relative to the fragility of life itself, and how even a light breeze can burst one. Some say they demonstrate how our dreams can float away from us or be popped in mid-flight.

A bubble meditation can leverage all of these ideas in a way that supports you to release what is no longer serving you. In this meditation, the bubble itself is just like a soap bubble, except for one important difference: its outer membrane is strong enough to hold whatever you place inside. It can get bigger and fuller, and still float on the air like a feather. All you need for this meditation is a quiet, comfortable place to sit, and your imagination. Here are the steps:

1.   Create in your mind's eye a giant bubble, floating in the air in front of you. It can be large enough to fit a whole person. Make it whatever size you want.

2.   One by one, bring to mind the conditions you would like to release from your life.

3.   One by one, transfer them from yourself to the bubble. Energetically extract them from inside you and give them over to the bubble. Imagine yourself handing them over—this is your conscious act of giving the issues away.

4.   When you have placed the last one into the bubble, take a deep breath in and peacefully exhale, blowing the bubble away from you. Do this several times until the bubble is so far away, it's become a tiny speck.

5.   In your mind's eye, reach way out there and pop it. As the bubble pops, trust that the things it contained have dissolved back into the Universe and they are no longer yours. Their molecules are being transmuted into a totally different substance that no longer has anything to do with you.

6.   Again, give some meditation time to what is going to flow into your life as a result of the release. What new state of mind and heart will be yours

now that you have released what wasn't working? Write them down to make them more concrete, and revisit them daily as a reminder of your focus on your new inner state.

Releasing People

It's likely that your relationships with some of the people in your life will no longer feel right. To feel 100 percent supported being your True Self, your inner circle and those people with whom you spend the most play/work time may have to shift. Those who were in your life at the beginning of this awakening are not *necessarily* the ones who will support you through the next part of your journey. Some people will evolve with you, others will not.

You arrived at this juncture because you're actively seeking more happiness and fulfillment in your life. You won't enjoy being with people whose behaviors and beliefs feel like the "old" you. If they are expressing from their own false-selves, their way of being will no longer feel good to you. Being in their presence will be uncomfortable. You will hear/feel your True Self taking issue with points-of-view they hold, and that you *used to hold,* because you now know better. You will likely feel a strange and growing distance between you and them, and it might not be clear how to respond to these feelings.

On the one hand, it will feel better to be distanced from what you know is a façade or what you have proven for yourself is an unfulfilling way of being. Yet on the other hand, you will probably feel some fear and sadness at the thought of not being with them anymore. The fear of being alone and/or the feelings of not having enough people who like and understand you around may be overwhelming at times.

Instead of leaving people where they are, allowing them to have their own experiences, you may even try to hang on, pulling them along with you. You may introduce them to this book (Yes, please do!), or workshops you've taken, or other things that helped you make the shift. Yet, for whatever reasons, they may not be able to go where you are going on the same timing, or with the same devotion and enthusiasm. Be prepared because these may even be the people closest to you.

I've experienced this. There have been times when it was clear that I had to create new relationships and routines that would support my ongoing evolution. I had to reconcile how I felt about the person and who they'd been in my life. I had to tiptoe and baby-step my way sometimes before I could willingly create true and lasting separation from them. Trusting that I, and the people I had released, would be okay, helped me feel secure and peaceful with these decisions when they were necessary. I also learned the difference between releasing someone physically from my life and releasing them energetically, meaning I stopped communicating and engaging with them, and they stopped communicating and engaging with me.

> *Releasing people who are not in alignment with you is a necessary and empowering step...*

Physical release is appropriate for people in whose presence you can no longer be. Perhaps there are people who are insensitive, critical, mean, or who don't honor your beliefs and wishes in certain aspects of your life. Perhaps it's not about how they treat you but how they treat themselves that is difficult for you to bear. Regardless, it's time for you to move on, making space for truer connections in your life. A physical release means you no longer interact with them—ever. You truly walk away. No confrontations or explanations are necessary; you simply hold fast to your decisions to be free of relationships that are more about your past than your future. In my experience, for these types of relationships, once I stopped communicating and engaging, so did they. As your vibration shifts, you attract people whose vibrations match.

For those family, friends, and colleagues with whom a connection is still reasonable, rewarding and loving, the release is different. I use an energetic release instead of a physical one. This means I release attachment to the idea that I need them in my life, or that I need them to be a certain way in my life, while I lovingly accept them in my life. I work on becoming neutral relative to everything about them. I still spend time with them, but I do so from my new place of Being. I allow them to "do life" in their own ways and be where they are in *their* Souls' evolution, which is right and perfect for them, and at the same time, not harmful to me or reflecting some self-abandonment on my part. I'm teaching myself that I don't have to react to their choices or beliefs. I don't have to see them as somehow needing fixing or de-programming. I let them and our relationships just BE.

I will also tell you that in cases where you have trouble deciding which release is best, you can just leave it alone and see how the relationship evolves over time. The people involved might shift themselves, which could close the Consciousness gap between you and make being in relationship more in alignment with your newer beliefs. Or you could continue to shift while they continue to do life their own way, and the gap widens. In that scenario, you may simply gravitate away from each other because your vibrations are no longer in alignment. However it happens, releasing people who are not in alignment with you is a necessary and empowering step in the process.

Some Final Thoughts on Release

I trust that in these various options, you find a couple that support you to make the **Shake Up!** Step fruitful and freeing. Regardless of which release technique you use, what really matters is that you truly let go of whatever it is you release. Don't pick the issue back up again. Don't reactivate its power in your psyche or persona. Don't start hanging out with that old friend who brought you down. You may have thoughts and feelings about the released issues and people come up here and there, but if you choose not to engage them, the effect of your efforts to release what no longer serves you will go deeper into you, making it more complete and long-lasting.

Also remember, a true release is rarely, if ever, a once-and-you're-done effort. The techniques/rituals help you ceremoniously and powerfully say "I'm done with this!" at a single point in time. It's maintaining the commitment to that choice over and over and over from that moment forward that enables you to transform your Consciousness over time.

I hope you noticed that I added my own touches to make the rituals 'mine.' I encourage you to do the same. If you love candles, incorporate them; if you have a special place that provides a meaningful backdrop for your release experience, go there; if you prefer to have a sacred companion act as witness as you engage the process, invite him/her. Make the release tools that you choose what they need to be to support you to free yourself from what is holding you back. Remember to keep it light, and where possible, make it energizing. You can laugh at yourself as part of the release; you can run along the beach flailing your arms and screaming at the waves as you release; you can sing off-key out loud about what you're wanting to release. It's up to you.

If your release in the **Shake Up!** Step is anything like mine, you will feel like you have let something go, and it will show back up again. This happened for me in my relationships, when people would call me intimidating or feel anger coming from me even when that's not what I was intending to convey. I was frustrated and sad at how often this would come up (mostly on my performance evaluations at work because people were too afraid to tell me to my face), in spite of all the work I was doing to make myself be different. I want you to know now that this Step may require more than a ritual or meditation. Even at my most committed, there were times when I needed outside help to get me to the next level.

When you consider how many of our blocks are in the subconscious, it's not difficult to understand why outside, objective help can be so crucial. These buried blocks of negative, conditioned patterns of beliefs and behaviors were established in us as youngsters. They can become so lodged, and their effects so pronounced and continual, as to convince us they are real, they are really the way the world works, and they are really us. When healing those kinds of emotional/spiritual issues, I knew I needed sage counsel to help me find, properly diagnose and heal them, before the release would be deep enough to be complete. The loving objectivity of an outsider, especially one adept at spiritual counseling (which I have found different and more successful than psychology or psychiatry), made a big difference in how I interpreted what was going on and why, as well as what I chose to do about it.

I have attended workshops to learn modalities to help myself; I've also invited spiritual directors, clairvoyants, Reiki masters, life coaches, Akashic Records experts, and others to provide perspective and guidance. In an ideal world, our connection to Divine Wisdom needs no such intermediary, and as I have released the hidden blocks within, I have directly felt and understood more of the Divine messages coming to me. They were always there; I just couldn't experience them through the muck and yuck in my Consciousness. Importantly, even now when I am the most clear in my life, I continue to engage the support of a Spiritual Master teacher and counselor, who helps me see myself at the deepest levels, and guides me on my continual journey to take my Consciousness and self-expression to the highest levels.

I encourage you to be open to inviting in the help you need to make the **Shake Up!** an ongoing and deeply freeing experience that enables you to express more of the **Magnificent Essence** that you are. We are Blessed to have masters all over the world whose life mission it is to shift the planet from fear to Love. Most of the ones I encounter are in the highest of integrity, and continue to be on this inner spiritual journey  themselves, even while they serve others. They have their own healing networks and activities, and they see themselves as support rather than substitutes—meaning they don't want you to be dependent on them for your unfoldment. They want to shepherd you to your own mastery-level engagement with your Consciousness and God, as well as the mystery, metaphysical nature and mysticism of life.

Of course, once you actually do take action towards release, you'll feel freer and emotionally lighter. Your outer expression will become softer, more optimistic, more fun, and/or more peaceful. Because your being-ness will have open spaces, you will find yourself wanting to try on new ways of expressing and experiencing. Explore and discover what feels better to you now. You'll be shaking up the idea of yourself—the answer to the question of "Who am I?" will be in a state of flux, and if you are willing to embrace the discomfort of the unknown, it will be exhilarating.

Step 3: MAKE UP! A NEW STORY OF YOU IN YOUR LIFE

So far, you've explored the old stories of your life. From your efforts in the **Wake Up!** Step, you've looked below the surface of these stories to see how and when they came to be, and to discern which ones are false measures of who you are in the world. You've looked at your life through a different lens and awakened *in* yourself a new or deepened awareness *of* yourself as a Divine Being.

Through your dance with your conscious and subconscious beliefs, behaviors, and bonds in the **Shake Up!** Step, you've gotten clear on the things that you are willing to be free of, and you've taken the first steps to release yourself from them. This has created some new and empty spaces in you and your life. Congratulations! You have now established a beautiful foundation on which to create life anew. You are now ready to be reborn into a truer expression of you that, through the Universal Spiritual Laws of Attraction and Reflection, will create a new, more Divine experience of your life. It's time for the **Make Up!** Step.

The **Make Up!** Step is the creation portion of the process. It's where you replace what you have released with something that serves you better. It's about crafting the next chapters of your life with conscious intention. It's a time to unleash your creativity and imagination. It's a space that is awaiting the wonder and delight of your inner child. It's about writing the new story of the way you intend to BE as the rest of your life unfolds.

I love the way this Rumi quote captures the underlying idea of this Step:

Don't be satisfied with stories, how things have gone with others... unfold your own myth... ~ Rumi

Rumi, whose full name is Jalāl ad-Dīn Muhammad Rūmî, was a 13th century Persian poet and Sufi mystic, whose writings are beloved in the U.S. and around the world. Some think of him as one of the most profound and influential spiritual writers of all time. What I love most about Rumi is the Love in his writings. I find myself smiling and feeling full of Grace when I engage with his poems for even brief periods of time. I find humor and delight, wisdom and insight into the whole Universe in his works. I also appreciate how his writings prod us into undertaking the journey of our lives with boldness, reverence, and faith.

This quote is actually a part of one of the last lines in a Rumi poem which has been entitled "Unfold Your Own Myth" by translators (Rumi didn't title his poems). Like all of his writings, there are layers of meaning in the individual lines, as well as the poem in its entirety. On the whole, the poem speaks to me about creativity, self-actualization, independence, and the mystery of seeking something big *within* oneself to enrich one's life.

Starting from the last word, "myth," defined loosely as legends, fables, and stories built on exaggerated truths—I think of the tales that make life seem bigger and richer than most people actually experience. Slaying dragons, fanciful lives created from a simple kiss, love at first sight, and patenting an idea that turns into billions of dollars. Even to the people living these legends, some aspects seem too good to be true. This potentially can leave the rest of us feeling like it can never happen that way for us, and the story becomes the next best thing to the actual experience. In this line, Rumi is admonishing us not to settle for a *re-telling* of something larger than life, but to go create and experience it for ourselves. It's about having the imagination to dream big, and cultivating the courage and self-confidence to transcend being

the dreamer to become the central character in the story. It's about each of us creating what legends are made of in our own lives. No more living vicariously through characters on the big screen or YouTube, on the "30 Under 30" list, in articles in *The Wall Street Journal*, or in mystery or romance novels. Make your own life so big, bold, and aspirational, as to be difficult to believe. Create for yourself something *worth* writing about, and rich enough to be told over and over.

Unfolding your own myth is about writing the story of how you will express the **Magnificent Essence** that you are. Who are you going to be, what will you do and why, who will you serve and how?

For me, the wounds and false-self had me expressing as drill-sergeant, judge, jury, executioner, guilty, shameful, hiding, fearful, and less-than, both with others and with myself. None of those expressions were from the *True* me, nor were they how I consciously intended to be. I was being run by negative conditioned patterns of belief and behavior from my past—the issues in the iceberg below the surface of me. Once I started healing the wounds that created the issues, I was able to shift to align with my True inner Self. This is the highest Consciousness of me that expresses as Unconditional Love (for myself and others), Peace, Abundance, and Joy.

As I breathe life into the **Make Up!** Step for myself, empowered with a deeper connection to myself as a Divine Being, I have been making entirely new decisions about every aspect of my life, re-writing my story into its own legendary reflection of my **Magnificent Essence**! My outer life experiences continue to reflect my inner shifts. Here are some examples of the aspects of the myth I am writing and unfolding:

- I don't strive and struggle for the things I want. The "effortless effort" that I trust is a demonstration of being a Divine Being is a concrete experience in my life.

- I have given up settling for things. What I *really want* shows up—in terms of relationships, opportunities, and situations.

- My ability to receive has increased, so more juicy goodness shows up. As I've healed the old ideas of being unlovable and unworthy, I am in alignment with the gifts that have always been a part of the Divine Promise.

- My capacity for expressing compassion and kindness, for myself and others, has increased. As a result, my impact on others has shifted as well. People now tell me they experience my presence as peaceful, playful, inspiring and free, rather than competitive, intimidating, angry, and resentful.

- I am taking bolder steps to play bigger and be more fearless. This book is the biggest example of overcoming the fear of persecution I used to subconsciously associate with using my voice in far-reaching ways.

- I go out by myself because I've let go of the idea that doing so says something bad about me as a companion or a date.

- I have taken drawing classes and continue to draw, though I'm far from being good at it. I just like the act of expressing my creativity.

- I'm learning to be a part of things without having to lead them, which I used to do to feel seen, accepted and respected.

- I laugh and play more. Laughing at myself is much easier and is also empowering.

- I work less and still feel accomplished and successful—somewhat because my definitions of what those words mean have changed. It's also because on my relativity scale, being accomplished and successful are actually not that important to me anymore. Fully being me trumps those any day!

- I no longer judge my mistakes so harshly. I acknowledge them with a more neutral heart, and quickly shift from feeling bad about the mistake to looking for the gift in the circumstance. I've always done a "search for the silver lining," as I called it, but I used to carry a lot of frustration, guilt, shame, sadness, resentment and anger around about every mistake. Those feelings and judgments made getting the gift feel more like a punishment.

- I'm willing to cancel appointments if my desires in the moment are different from those when I originally made the plans—which means I'm being true to me and less worried about pleasing everyone else.

There are two ways I suggest everyone begin the **Make Up!** Step. Start by re-writing yourself into the lead role in the legend of your life. As the lead, the star, you are the most important character. How you're feeling, what you're thinking, what you want and don't want, are critical to the story unfolding to its fullest epic potential. Every scene is enriched when the aspects of that scene revolve around you.

If you're like most people, the false-self has made *your* life mostly about "them" and "that" where you appear almost like an extra. Your purpose is about creating stability, opportunity, support, excitement, possibility, achievement, and love for your spouse, your kids, your boss, your staff, your pets, your community responsibilities, and on and on. The list is long, never to be completed, and what really serves *you* is rarely on it. IF you make the list at all, you're at the bottom, generally only when everything else has been done for everyone else. Like the photo above, the scales you're trying to balance have everything on them *but you.*

As you engage with the Steps of **Living Happy to Be ME!**, you should be becoming more and more aware of how, when and why you deny your existence and betray your needs and desires to make sure everyone else is taken care of first. It's likely that you are expressing what you were taught about where "Godliness" comes from. Something about being selfless, about giving yourself to others in service, about being humble and surrendered. Unfortunately, this is not an expression of yourself as **Magnificent Essence**. The core teaching of this book is that as Essence of the Divine, you already are Godly, and so no outer self-denial, self-betrayal, or self-abandonment is necessary to prove yourself thus. It's time you edit this part of your tale into non-existence.

It's time for you to help your True Self emerge so you can remember that you are worthy of every good thing that you give to others. It's not just okay, but absolutely necessary to fill yourself up, if you truly want to serve others. This is where you must start in the new story of your life. It's time to balance the giving scales so that you are prominently a receiver.

Best-selling author, acclaimed speaker, and powerful business leader Lisa Nichols makes this point beautifully with a cup and a saucer as a metaphor for ourselves. As she's filling the cup with water, she asks the audience, when they think it's okay to give of themselves to others. Some people say it's time when the cup is half full; others say when the cup is almost full; still others say to give when the cup is full to the brim. But the wise answer is that we are best able to give when our cup is *overflowing*, and not before. If we do so before, we actually deplete ourselves in the process—meaning we give to others to our own detriment. That is not what is intended by the teachings of selfless service.

Give yourself permission to *leap* into the starring role in your life and begin right away to tip the scales in favor of you. Help people in your life understand and accept that *you* matter to *you*, and you will **Make Up!** a story that features exceptional levels of healthy and responsible selfishness!

Remember that your life is always going to be a reflection of your relationship with yourself. As you get clear on the *inside* that you count, and start to express that Truth, the outer world will become a mirror image of that expression. As part of *that* awareness and expression, you will naturally write new expression into your story. I hope you noticed in my list above how I became more nurturing to myself, more open to my creative expression, more comfortable making decisions that supported me even if others might feel let down. My whole outer world has shifted because I follow what calls to and pleases me. And I do it in love and compassion, not in judgement, competition, and resentment.

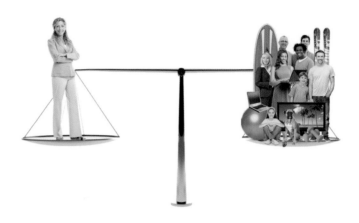

One example that I love sharing is that in almost every case, when I cancel a prior commitment, the other person is generally grateful. I've actually let them off the hook. They admit that they're too tired, or overbooked, or the idea is just not that enticing to them anymore, and they would have cancelled themselves but they didn't feel comfortable doing so. They're clearly in the old energy of pleasing others. But the synchronous beauty continues. As I express what healthy and responsible selfishness looks like, they *feel* it. My self-care touches the part of them that desperately wants more self-care of their own. They get a glimpse into how they can make a shift in *their* life, and a ripple effect is born! So even by serving myself, I end up serving them too.

> **M**aking *yourself the most important thing in your life is a natural aspect of acknowledging being in alignment with* your **Magnificent Essence.**

Think about the opportunities like this that are calling to you. In HeartMath, the concept of giving to everyone else while ignoring ourselves is called "over-care." Where in your life are you loaning money, doing chores, taking on work assignments, resolving conflicts, overloading yourself with projects, or preventing those around you from making mistakes or failing that would fit under the concept of over-care? The only one who can balance those scales is you.

Making yourself the most important thing in your life is a natural aspect of acknowledging being in alignment with your **Magnificent Essence**. It means fully embodying and living the belief that you are already that which you seek. You can let go of the need to seek fulfillment, pleasure, acceptance, acknowledgement, encouragement, recognition or any other validation or approval from others as a means to feel good about yourself. It doesn't mean that you aren't grateful when any of these expressions come from outside sources. It also doesn't mean that you don't accept them when they are offered. I'm talking about the energy underneath the gratitude and acceptance. That energy inside you will shift from receiving these expressions as something you *need* to have, to being something that is *nice* to have. You'll know that the outside is simply mirroring what you're already doing to yourself for yourself, rather than filling an empty spot in your heart.

> You cannot ever be filled up by external experiences.
> Focusing *within* is the way fulfillment happens,
> and it starts with *you fulfilling yourself*.

The second foundational aspect of the **Make Up!** Step is to shift your model of creation. I touched on this earlier, but it's worth going a little deeper with it. This is about demonstrating that you know the inner realm of yourself—how you think and feel about yourself and your place in the world—as the key to creating your outer experience. Remember the Law of Reflection: what is going on inside you will be reflected outside of you.

Here's how it can work: You believe that achieving success is about starting with the end in mind. You create a mental and/or emotional attachment to something out in the distance, such as a goal, and then you create the means to achieve that goal. You pursue the goal as if creation of it starts with doing something. Ultimately, you're operating using a DO-HAVE-BE "model for creation" that goes like this: you DO things, to HAVE things, to BE (or FEEL) a certain way. For example:

- You work hard (DOingness) to HAVE many accomplishments/rewards/recognition, so you can BE successful/honorable/appreciated.

- You try to please others (DOingness), so you can HAVE their friendship/love/respect/loyalty/approval, so you can BE happy.

- Take a moment now and look for how you are creating your life with this model. You can probably think of several examples and keep the list going on and on.

Here's the thing—what is inherent in this model is *lack*. You are doing things to experience something you feel you lack. You believe that once you no longer lack this thing, your inner state will improve and you'll BE better off. But you can't create to your highest potential when you are coming from a place of lack. Lack attracts more lack. I am clear that this is why I often felt a let-down right after a major success—the subconscious feelings of less-than, unworthy, and/or unlovable that were inside me could not be overcome by any of the external accomplishments or successes. Have you ever noticed this experience in your life?

The problem as I see it is that using this model over and over has conditioned you to create backwards. You have to start from the place of already BEing whatever it is you believe you want. The BE part of the creation model needs to happen first.

> *You can't create to your highest potential when you are coming from a place of lack.*

The Steps of **Living Happy to Be ME!** help you shift into creating from a deep connection to your Divine State of Being FIRST.

Then you use that as the foundation for what you do and what you attract (or have). This is the way you can add Divine Power into the story of your life. This is how you enable your Highest Consciousness (your Soul) to deliver you to your highest potential. This is how you can be more conscious of the signal you are sending into the world—your energetic vibration—and therefore, anticipate what will be coming to you as a result.

This is the way Universal Law works in your life. You align with your **Magnificent Essence**… as a result, you are connected to the realm of Source Energy… as a result, you are Divinely guided and supported to manifest your intentions… as a result, Ease, Peace and Grace become routine experiences in your life… as a result, your life is more sweet, more fulfilling and more fun. *Everything* becomes more possible as it is fueled and supported from the realm of Source Energy, and as you connect to that Source within.

The model for creating the life you want is BE-DO-HAVE. When you manifest using this model, you choose to BE in your Divine State of Being, and then trust and allow that State to influence and be the basis for what you choose to DO, so you can HAVE (attract) what you want. The other wonderful thing that happens when you use this model, is you feel more abundant all the time. You can see where you actually don't need to do anything more to have that feeling you want. You realize that perhaps that thing that might have seemed so important, isn't really worth having that much at all—not because you don't want it, but because you already feel its presence abundantly in your life. It's coming from inside of you!

Here are some examples of affirmative statements that express how you can bring the BE-DO-HAVE creation model to life in your life:

- I will BE in connection with the Peace of ME, so I DO *whatever* I do with Divine Peace as my vibration, and have abundant Peace reflected back to me in my relationships, home, and business.

- I will BE in connection with the Love of ME, to vibrate Love as I do *whatever* I do, so I can have Unconditional Love deeply infused in my relationships and my self-expression.

- I will BE in connection with the Joy of ME to vibrate in Joy, attract joyful experiences and relationships, and literally, swim in happiness, always.

Check-in

This is a good time for you to try this shift on. Are you able to identify how you are creating in your life? Can you follow the pattern within yourself? Pick a goal that you have been working toward, and follow the steps below. For example, let's say your goal is to get a degree.

What are you DOing to accomplish this goal? Examples: Taking classes, working a summer job, studying hard, playing less, postponing getting married and having children.

_____

_____

_____

_____

_____

_____

_____

_____

What will you HAVE when you accomplish this goal? Examples: More respect in my field, more job opportunities, higher income.

_____

_____

_____

_____

_____

_____

_____

_____

_____

What will you BE when you accomplish this goal? Examples: I will be more successful, happier, more financially safe/stable.

_____

_____

_____

_____

_____

_____

_____

_____

_____

_____

Now see if you can shift it around so the BEingness comes first. Examples: I am BEing aligned with the successful and joyful nature of my True self, so that as I'm DOing the tasks to get my degree, I HAVE an abundance of successful and joyful experiences.

_____

_____

_____

_____

_____

_____

_____

_____

Can you feel the difference? In the BE-DO-HAVE version, you are starting from an acknowledgement that what you seek is already a part of who you are. You are emphatically making it the foundation of your goal achievement. You are setting yourself up to accomplish the various tasks that are part of the overall goal, already believing and affirming you will be successful and happy along the way.

Feel how when you make the shift to BE-DO-HAVE, you start from an inner place of abundance, rather than lack. Can you connect with that place within you? If this feels difficult to grasp, allow that to be okay, and don't dwell on the difficulty. Just keep applying the principles as you continue to dance with the Steps of **Living Happy to Be ME!**. As you put them into practice on a moment-by-moment, day-to-day basis, you will feel deeper into it; you will get insights into whether you're in the Divine State for creation, or in your human state. The former will feel expansive and empowering, even with the unknowns; the latter will feel limiting and heavy, and the unknowns will likely intensify these feelings.

Some ideas on story-writing

Writing a new story for the rest of your life may feel daunting—the rest of your life is a long time to map out all at once. But this Step doesn't have to be difficult or overwhelming. How you experience it is up to you. If you have engaged deeply with the previous two Steps, you should feel freer to dream from a blank slate than you have before. You should be in a place of a growing inner void, where you are less likely to hem yourself in by old ideas, expectations, and commitments that you have outgrown. I'm hoping there is excitement and hopefulness welling up inside you.

Allow yourself to revel in the idea of writing your story from a clean slate that you get to create.

If you feel fear, that's okay. You are in the process of releasing old stories of a smaller, more inhibited version of you, and you may feel resistance coming from that version. If so, be peaceful and loving with it, as you would if you were dealing with a wounded child. Tell that fearful version of yourself that all is well. Go inward and ask the fear what message it is wanting you to understand. Allow yourself to get the message, come to a more peaceful place and then get started. You may choose to go back and do more releasing in the **Shake Up!** Step. That's great! **Living Happy to Be ME!** means you revisit the Steps as many times as it takes to embody the principles so you have more of what you want throughout your life.

The best time to engage with this Step is when you can feel desire and joy thinking about it. Allow yourself to revel in the idea of writing your story from a clean slate that you get to create. No more pleasing others or doing what social consciousness dictates is appropriate or acceptable. Here are some ideas that may help you get started more easily:

- While it's great to have some idea of where you want to go in the big picture, you don't have to start with the rest of your life in mind. It's not necessary to fully know the end at the beginning. Remember the heart and soul of this Step is that you make the story all about you and what you want. You get to choose the timeframe that feels right. It could be the rest of the year; you could also just start with the rest of the day.

- Other than having intentions for the big outcomes, it's best if you stay detached from the nitty-gritty details. This is a chance to embrace flexibility. There are many paths to the same place. Allow Divine Mind to co-create the path of ease to your destination by getting clear on what you want without getting attached to how you will get it. For example, when I started rewriting my story, I knew I wanted to serve through some sort of "social ministry," but I wasn't sure if I wanted to get another masters degree or certifications in some specific modality. I focused on the end result being that I was 'sharing wisdom and love to help others experience love and peace.' That has included teaching, writing, speaking, and hosting so far, and it continues to unfold.

- Boldness counts—think big. It's your story—make it as fanciful, romantic, fun, and easy-going as you desire. Dream in vivid colors, and imagine experiencing your highest potential. This is where I sometimes felt the old ideas of limitation coming up inside me. I could see myself only going so far in terms of leading or creating. It was through the attempts to write the new story that I uncovered lingering aspects of the false self to release. I would still capture the bigger, bolder, new story, while I went through the process to do the healing and release. You should do the same.

- Make yourself the star. Think about how you want the others in your life to relate to, serve, support, connect with, collaborate with, honor, and love *you.* How do you want to feel when you spend time in relationship with others?

- Remember to think in terms of the BE-DO-HAVE model. The story should capture the Being nature of you as its foundation. For example, no matter what I am pursuing at a given moment relative to where I'm intending to go in my life, I stay centered in the **BE**ingness that I wish to experience: Peace, Love, Joy and Freedom. The **Magnificent Essence** of me. Anchoring in that as "home," I build the rest of the story staying true to my True self.

> **A**llow yourself to be in the creative and expressive nature of the heart, and make it perfect to be abstract, messy and creative.

Leave the rational, logical mind out of it. You're not trying to convince anyone else. Your story doesn't have to appeal to anyone else. So you don't have to make all the dots connect and tie it up in a neat little bow. Allow yourself to be in the creative and expressive nature of the heart, and make it perfect to be abstract, messy and creative. This is where dream books and vision boards can come in handy—they rely more on imagery than words to express your desires. You can go deeply into the right brain and heart.

It might be a good idea to keep your new story a personal project that you don't share. People will be noticing your shifts by now, and they may be uncomfortable with the new you. Remember that their reactions to things outside of them are about them, and not you, but you may be in an uncomfortable position of receiving their junk. If you feel the need to seek approval of others for the story you are creating, check-in and see what part of your old, potentially subconscious self needs to be healed and released. Explore that and see how the need to share your new story diminishes.

Ultimately, rewriting your story means that in the "right here right now," *you get to choose*. You get to choose how you want to see yourself. You get to choose to whose voice you listen. You get to choose what determines your choices. You get to choose how to explore what you want. You get to choose your purpose and how to express it. You get to choose who is in and who is out of your life. You get to choose how you will be different from this moment forward, so your whole life can be different in the future.

Once you wake up, you can never really go back to sleep. Once you notice that change is necessary, it's emotionally painful to ignore the need for change. Once you awaken and claim your True Self spiritually, it's very painful to ignore that aspect of who you are.

What an amazing opportunity! What a gift you are giving yourself! As you embrace the depth and breadth of this Step, your life experiences will evolve to reflect your evolving inner story of the Love, Peace, Joy and Freedom that you are. Even as you experience things that are *not* what you want from time to time, you will respond differently. You will notice yourself calling yourself back into alignment with the Divine Truth about you. You will look for what needs to be released, and you will rewrite the story that is evolving through that moment. You will find the good —the Divine Wisdom, Divine Guidance and Divine Love—in all your experiences, and you'll keep moving forward demonstrating your Freedom from the past. This is the kind of Freedom that only an *inner* journey can give you. This is the kind of Freedom you deserve. This is the *true* Freedom that's worth fighting for.

In this state of Freedom, you create your personal plan for continuing the journey higher into your Consciousness and deeper into the Truth of who you are. This is where the 4th Step of **Living Happy to Be ME!** begins.

Step 4: TAKE UP! THE REINS AND GO LIVE IT!

By now, I'm affirming that you can see these **4 Steps** as a concrete way to change your life, and that living them is about creating a lifestyle. It doesn't start with changing your environment. **Living Happy to Be ME!** is about you and what's going on *inside* you. If you want your life to be different, *you* have to be different. Once you change you, the rest will shift more easily and more permanently. Once you make inner shifts to be more of the Essence of you, it will feel more natural to make different choices in your various circumstances so the circumstances align more with Truth. As you choose differently, your life unfolds differently.

This is where the rubber meets the road. This is where you ground your Spiritual Self within your human experience, and co-create your life from wholeness as an integrated Spiritual-Human person. It means making a commitment to stay awake, claim Truth, choose wisely, and take action—over and over and over, day-in and day-out, 24-7-365. Take up the reins, commit to your reborn version of you, and create the practices that support your realization of your full potential. This Step helps you be **Living Happy To Be ME!** for the rest of your days!

Get busy livin', or get busy dyin'.
~ Andy Dufresne

This quote by lead character Andy Defresne in the 1994 film *Shawshank Redemption* has helped me remember there is no in-between place. I'm either living fully, or dying slowly. I get to choose. The same is true for you. You must make a *conscious* choice to live fully now, and then repeat that choice over and over throughout each new day. Consciously choosing to live fully means you are on a continual journey of exploration into new frontiers for the full and vibrant expression of yourself. You consciously commit to putting the **Essence** of you into all of your life. You refuse to die with the sweet and powerful bits of you still trapped inside in the prison of the ego's false self.

> You refuse to die with the sweet and powerful bits of you still trapped inside in the prison of the ego's false self.

Through the **Take Up!** Step, you ensure you are living fully because you use this Step to create the habits, practices, and support structure that bring your new vision to fruition over time. It's how you ensure that you embody all you have remembered and uncovered as you worked with this book.

The wisdom takes root as it is nurtured in action. The wisdom enables transformation as it is nurtured in action. The wisdom works for you as you work with it.

The **Take Up!** Step enables you to breathe real, tangible life into your ideas for your present and future. This Step helps you stay awake and keep dancing through the evolution of your Soul. It's how you "stand and deliver!" as my friend and fellow transformational coach, Gary de Rodriguez, would say. You stand for what you know is True and you deliver yourself into what you truly want.

This Step is how you lovingly continue to practice what you're learning until it becomes second-nature. This is the *Dancing Your Soul Lightstyle* that is the subtitle of this book. Think about the times you've tried to grow a new habit. Recall the dedication it took to shift away from old patterns and help something better take root. Perhaps you experienced some back-sliding or what appeared to be stagnation. Even with encouragement from those around you, the ultimate responsibility for keeping yourself energized and focused landed on you.

Think about any new skill you've wanted to learn, like how to speak a new language or manage your finances; how to skateboard, draw, or play the piano; how to dance, use a new technology, sew or cook; or even how to do origami or rodeo wrangling. First, you have to understand the details and nuances of *how* to do it. Then you have to do it. The more you choose to *do* it routinely and frequently, the quicker you *embody* the how.

It is the same with the **Living Happy To Be ME!** process. You are responsible for your progression toward your highest good, and you will be the one who gets you through inner questioning, a wavering commitment, feelings of stagnation, lack of demonstration, or other challenging situations that may arise. It's not a one-time-and-you're done exercise. It is an ongoing process. This Step is where you claim your support structure, *in advance.*

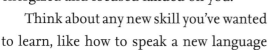

We are what we repeatedly do. Excellence then, is not an act, but a habit. ~ Aristotle

Aristotle's words capture the central theme of this Step. While your conscious commitment is a concrete foundation, your transformation is an *ongoing process* and it doesn't happen all at once, and certainly not overnight. So it's time to start asking— how are you going to get yourself from your starting point to each subsequent point along your journey?

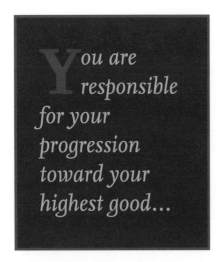

You are responsible for your progression toward your highest good...

Ask yourself, how will you turn the new habits you chose in Steps 2 and 3, into ongoing practices that will support you best, as you "get busy living" anew? How will you smoothly transition from the old game of struggle and strife to real living, which is about effortless effort? How will you incorporate new routines that support more ease and peace blossoming into your experiences? How will you phase out interactions with people who are not aligned with your vibration anymore? In order to continue your evolution, you will want to incorporate situations, additional teachings, and ongoing healing, *and* you will want to be surrounded and supported by loving people who are as committed to walking in Truth as you are.

The **Take Up!** Step is your chance to consciously choose the ways you will support the ongoing shift in your vibrational energy to attract the life you want. You will find dozens of ways to explore and create this support structure. I invite and encourage you to be open to anything and everything that shows up or calls to you. Check-in to see how something is resonating and whether you feel expanded or contracted when considering it or when experiencing it.

Note that this 'check-in' is not about your rational and logical reasons for or against something—in other words, it's not a head experience. You should be checking-in with your heart and it's intuitive Soul-level guidance by connecting with the *feeling* of the idea. For example, you may *feel* a warmth in your chest or gut, a tickle in your cheeks, or notice a smile coming to your face as your initial reaction to something new. I encourage you to trust and say "yes" to that before your head engages to tell you all the reasons you shouldn't want to try it. Bless the feelings as your intuitive inner guidance, and move forward in trust. I know it can feel risky to allow something other than your brain to guide you, but it's time. This is an opportunity to practice the "If it feels good, do it" method for choosing, trusting that your intuitive self is a more True guide to your highest potential than your intellect alone.

It's the same if your initial reaction is an inner feeling of contraction, like shrinking away, or of anxiety in your chest or gut. Trust that as your intuitive inner guidance giving you a "not for me" before your head chimes in to tell you all the reasons you *should* do something. It's okay to consider something, check-in with your heart, and then opt-out.

Know that not all yeses will be forever and not all nos will mean never. You'll create new awarenesses as you continue with your **Living Happy To Be ME!** unfoldment, and as you do so, you'll also connect to the energy of what kinds of things fit better, and what feels long versus short-term. The key is to stay focused on how the experience contributes to your ongoing awakening, and then courageously choose.

Adopting New Beliefs and Behaviors

There are many perspectives and plenty of guidance on how to effectively create a new habit. I'm going to share one of my favorites from author and expert on human behavior, productivity, habits, and creative work, Gregory Ciotti. Greg advocates what he calls "behavior chains," which basically suggests that you connect your new behavior to something that is already a healthy part of your routine. You create an "if-then" relationship between the old routine and the desired new habit, and the routine becomes a trigger for the new behavior. Isn't this great! Your old and new come together in a way where one helps serve the other! You use the situational context to be successful instead of relying solely on your willpower. According to Greg, multiple studies confirm this as effective.

Know that not all yeses will be forever and not all nos will mean never.

For example, let's say you want to stop eating sugar at lunchtime. Instead of declaring you will never eat sugar again, and then fight the urge every time it comes up, you could create an "implementation intention" related to when the sugar urge is pressuring you. This commitment works like this:

- At lunch (routine)...

- When I crave sugary treats (old trigger)...

- I will have a piece of fruit instead (new desired behavior).

Here are some examples of how I used behavior chain implementation in my evolution of going from low-vibration to higher-vibration self-image:

- In conversations with colleagues (routine), when I get questions (old trigger), if I feel old feelings of anxiety and fear, I will not engage until I take a deep breath, and remind myself I am safe and all is well. I will respond when my inner energy feels neutral (new desired belief and behavior).

- In conversations with family (routine), when I feel the need to explain or defend my position (old trigger), I will tell the other person I accept their point of view and let go of the need to be understood or to be right (new desired belief and behavior).

- During relaxation time (routine), when I'm craving a snack (old trigger), I will check in on whether the feeling is really about food or something else I need to give myself, and see if the food is really what I want (new behavior).

Again, the gift in this process is that you get to be more conscious of the triggers for your old beliefs and behaviors, and in which routines they are embedded. You might be amazed at how many times and ways you are being triggered without being consciously aware that it's happening. By being more aware of the triggers, you can alter your responses, and enable lasting change to take place in your life.

Surrounding Yourself With the Right People

The choice to include a person in your life in a significant or intimate way will be different now. You will *feel* "right" connections more than you will intellectually choose them. You might find that the people you are most attracted to will shift. You might find that now, you have spiritual or "deep" conversations with work colleagues, when you never used to feel comfortable doing so. That's because you are shifting your vibration, and you will attract that which is a reflection of what is going on inside you. Perhaps those work colleagues were always willing to and interested in engaging in such conversations, but you were not free enough or willing to be vulnerable or authentic enough to do so.

As you accept and love more of yourself, people and situations will show up that feel more loving and accepting of you exactly as you are. As you slow down and spend more time BEing, you'll notice people who honor the same thing in you and in themselves, and it will feel natural to be in relationship with them. It will become easier and easier to surround yourself with the right people. They will simply show up. As you continue to go higher and deeper into your True Self, your relationships will reflect that which you are committed to expressing. When you express from your **Magnificent Essence** of Peace, Love, Joy, and Freedom, you will attract and experience those dynamics in the people and situations in your life.

Essential Practices

Again, it's not enough to know the Truth intellectually as a body of knowledge. You must act on it, over and over and over, until it becomes your default way of responding to the situations in your life. You want to embody it. Think of embodiment as a state in which there is no separation between a situation arising and you acting on it.

For example, when you brush your teeth in the morning, you don't stop and think of each step of that process individually. Similarly, when you take a route

to school or work, you're almost on auto-pilot. These automatic-response moments are because you have embodied the knowledge associated with each situation. You do them without thinking about what's involved. We all live our lives with these collections of embodiments that combine to get us through our days. Remember, this is where we started—unraveling your previously rooted and embodied beliefs and behaviors to find out what has been driving you from beneath the surface.

Embodiment of this new information is about replacing your old routine or 'knee-jerk' reactions to the situations in your life, with new ways of being. These new ways must be grounded in the spiritual aspect of you and in harmony with the spiritual laws of the universe. This is the heart of the **Take Up!** Step.

The second half of this book, "Free Your Lightstyle," suggests close to 80 ways to get into the groove of change and transformation. Some of them are from my experiences, and others were collected from people just like you who have explored ways to make positive shifts in their beliefs and behaviors. There's a variety, and in general, they are individual, one-time experiences! Here, I'd like to emphasize three of my favorites for *ongoing* practice. By that, I mean I strongly recommend you incorporate them into your daily experiences to help you embody the wisdom —FOREVER.

Growing the self-awareness, self-acceptance, and self-love that we've been exploring in this book requires an ongoing cultivation and nurturing. I liken it to tending the roses in my garden—the more care and prayer I shower on them, the more full bushes and colorful, fragrant blossoms with which they Bless me. This is what spiritual practice is. Continued engagement in the practice is how the practice helps you blossom into the fullness of your Spiritual-human potential.

If you are on a committed journey to having more happiness, fulfillment and success, these next three activities will serve you well no matter how frequently you do them. But this is also a case of more is more. The more you choose to experience them in earnest, the more you will benefit!

Meditate Daily

Meditation is the foundation of my spiritual practice. The silence within meditation is a place of mental rest and rejuvenation, as well as a way to stay connected to the **Magnificent Essence** within myself. This aspect of me is where my Truest guidance for my earthly unfoldment can be heard, and listening well requires the noisy background chatter in my head to recede. Meditation is key to that.

I have been meditating almost daily for over a decade. I am trained in transcendental meditation, and I also use guided meditation recordings and walking Japa (recitation of a mantra) when I want to experience meditation differently. I like to attend group "sits" and have also been to multi-day silent meditation retreats. Over time, I have created such a devoted relationship with meditation that I often crave it in the same way that I can crave chocolate or sushi!

If you have never tried to meditate, it's time to start; if you have tried and stopped, it's time to start again. Remember that hearing the intuitive inner voice is part of being in alignment with your inner Divine Nature and the guidance and support that await you there. Quieting the chatter in the conscious mind is the best way to enable yourself to do that. When you add the physiological benefits of meditation to the spiritual one, it's really a no-brainer. There's more on meditation in "Quiet Your Mighty Mind" later in the book. Just do yourself a favor now and commit to incorporating meditation into your life, no matter what it takes to hone your ability to do so.

> **P**lay doesn't have to mean goofing off and doing nothing.

Play More

I also encourage you to look for ways to be more playful every day. A play practice is a great way for you to reinforce the idea that you do *not* need to fill all of your time with pursuit of accomplishments, credentials, recognition and reward. It's a reminder that play is a part of Divine creation, and it helps your evolution to disengage from your "busy-ness" and lighten up about making everything in your life so serious. Fun and free-spiritedness are not equal to irresponsibility and frivolousness.

In the pure energy of the inner child are the wellsprings of imagination, innocence and wonder. Your childlike imagination can open doors to whole

new worlds for you to explore, in work and play, making it easier for you to make concrete shifts that support your ongoing evolution. The innocence of the child can help you greet every situation with a blank slate, which allows you to be more present with the experience, rather than doing it as you always have. Activating your child's sense of wonder will help you marvel at everything—even the things you previously would have thought mundane, like brushing your teeth or driving to work.

It's important to know that a desire to "play" doesn't *have to* mean goofing off and doing nothing. It also doesn't necessarily mean organized sports, which can be so serious and high-stakes, as to have zero pure play involved at all. You can make your play experience what it needs to be to help you be whole and present. I nurture my inner desire for more playtime proactively, and by applying my adult reasoning about timing and kinds of activities to what I choose, I ensure I'm present with the desire. So I might take a break from my office and take a bubble bath or paint a little in the middle of the day. Or I might look at how I can activate the *energy* of play inside myself while I'm doing whatever "work" I'm doing. Most of the time, I can make this connection simply by using my imagination (mentioned above) to create a new relationship with the old task. The other way to make the connection is to do what you love, what brings you the most joy, most of the time, and you'll feel like you're playing even when you're deeply engaged with the associated tasks.

Laugh a Lot

Laughter has been studied for decades for its therapeutic effects. Back in the 1960's, Dr. William Fry, a noted psychiatrist at Stanford University and considered the father of 'gelotology' (the science of laughter), began studying the physiological effects of laughter. His experiments demonstrated that laughter stimulates the body's major systems, that even fake laughter can produce a positive effect, and that laughter is a natural painkiller (it stimulates the body to release endorphins).

> **I** say laugh often, laugh deep, laugh proud!

You may have heard of Norman Cousins. In 1979, he published the celebrated *Anatomy of an Illness*, in which he describes his personal suffering from a potentially fatal and painful disease. Cousins documented that along with a positive attitude that incorporated love, faith, and hope, he used regular intervals of laughter induced by Marx Brothers films to help himself. "I made the joyous discovery that ten minutes of genuine belly laughter had an anesthetic effect and would give me at least two hours of pain-free sleep," he reported. His story inspired a number of subsequent research projects, and the long and short of it is that laughter really is a phenomenal form of medicine!

Laughter yoga was created by a medical doctor in Mumbai, India some 16 years later based on the mounting cause-effect relationship between laughter and healing. Since its creation, the therapeutic effects of laughter yoga have also been proven. It relieves stress and boosts immunity, creativity, and self-confidence, among other benefits. Today, it is practiced formally by thousands of clubs in more than 80 countries around the world.

I say laugh often, laugh deep, laugh proud! I am so committed to living that mantra, I've incorporated laughter into my spiritual practice through improvisational comedy and laughter yoga. In fact, I'm a certified laughter yoga leader and I use it in my **Living Happy To Be ME!** workshops. You simply cannot laugh too much. The central idea is "mirthful" laughter, which is about light-hearted, uplifting laughter. In laughter yoga, we do this without use of the left-brain, which means it's not about joke-telling or having something to "laugh at." It's just about cultivating a feeling of wanting to laugh and then laughing. To maximize the therapeutic effect, 20-minute sessions are recommended.

So whether you watch light-hearted comedy programs, join a laughter yoga club, or take an improv comedy class, get laughing, and make a conscious choice to get some extended laughter in every day! Most importantly, when you free yourself to laugh *at yourself*, the benefits go even deeper.

Remember, this is about you as a *whole* Spiritual-Human person living an integrated life. There can no longer be different faces of you for the different pieces of your life. The idea that you can have a you for school/work, a you for social experiences, a different you for intimate situations, and a different you as soccer captain or volunteer leader, is part of the old energy of false beliefs that said you couldn't be the same you everywhere you go. Use the **Take Up!** Step to ensure your old beliefs in fragmentation and separation are not influencing how you show up in your life going forward.

As you apply the **4-Steps** of **Living Happy to Be ME!,** you will go deeper into your self-awareness, self-acceptance and self-love, which means you'll also go higher into your Consciousness. Feel your way through the internal feedback you get on how you're doing. Go with the ebbs and flows. Don't take it so seriously as to make it a chore. Allow things to move and grow as you move and grow. Delight in knowing that you are being the master of your life, rebirthing yourself into your birthright of Peace, Love, Joy and Freedom!

Putting it All Together

Now that we've covered the **4 Steps** individually, it's time to look at how they integrate so you can apply them successfully in your life. The **Living Happy to Be ME!** process is not linear though we've covered it that way so far. We explored the **4 Steps** this way to make it easier for you to get clear on the important elements of each **Step** and how to put them into practice. You don't *actually* start and finish each **Step** individually before moving on to the next one. I like to think of the process as diving into a many-layered cake. I prefer the cake metaphor to the peeling-back-an-onion metaphor because I want to think of all aspects of my life as having the potential to be sweet, rich, and beautiful. I don't feel any of those things in association with an onion!

Imagine yourself as the cake, and imagine your movement through the **4 Steps** as a "Spiral of Awakening and Transformation" that helps you get below the surface layer of icing, to the first layer of cake, and each subsequent layer of cake and icing beneath. And deep into the cake, lies the best part—the rich, delicious center. This is the best part of the cake, and no matter how many layers you must go through to get there, it's worth the trip, because you know that's what you really want, and why you started eating the cake in the first place.

On the surface of the cake is the beautiful icing, your outer covering, which you have created and are showing to the world. Perhaps it is reflecting the **Magnificent Essence** of you. Perhaps it's showing you the masks you're wearing to have others see you a certain way. Perhaps it's reflecting some belief you have about yourself that is from the false self. As you go through the **4 Steps**, you uncover what is real and what is false. You get to layers where the cake feels dense and the outer experience of whatever is beneath the surface is difficult. Perhaps finances are tough, clarity about your purpose is missing, job satisfaction is low, relationships are unfulfilling, there are more questions than answers. Perhaps things are relatively good, but you just feel uneasy all the time, like something important is missing. Perhaps things are great, and you feel troubled that despite that, you don't feel settled and fulfilled. Perhaps this is reflecting stuck energy from past experiences that you deemed good or bad. Whatever the circumstance, the parts that don't *feel* right and True, what I call denseness, reflect that something in you is no longer serving you. You can apply the **4 Steps** all at once:

- What is the **Wake Up!** call in the situation? What is the Truth you need to remember about yourself as **Magnificent Essence**? What is being reflected from you, to you, about you for your highest good?

- What do you need to **Shake Up!** in your ideas about yourself or your place in the world, and what can you release that doesn't fit anymore?

- How can you **Make Up!** a new story with yourself as the star, and with you fully accepting and loving you? What's included and excluded in your story going forward? How does the story set you up to be the whole, integrated, Spiritual-human that you are?

- What do you need to do to **Take Up!** the reins and live anew, from the healed, more spiritually-aligned you? How will you continue on the new path to raising your Consciousness and experiencing your true and lasting happiness?

The **Magnificent Essence** *of you— expansive, creative, loving, energizing, full...*

Are you seeing how you can do this over and over and over again as new situations arise? Let's say you move forward with big enthusiasm from the first application of the **4 Steps**. For a time, you're smoothly sailing along, smiles on your face and in your heart. You hit some stormy seas. Maybe something major happens on the outside like the loss of a relationship or job; maybe you just feel an awareness from the inside that something is not right. From your more awake and aligned place, you apply the **4 Steps** again. You go another layer deeper into the layer cake of your life to find Truth to manage the situation. You find more density—what is *not* Truth—and you apply the **4 Steps**. The density is released and you experience the sweet, rich, beautiful you. You are then better able to deal with the situation at hand from a place of the **Magnificent Essence** of you— expansive, creative, loving, energizing, full—rather than the limiting, mundane, fearful, and debilitating false-self. And it continues like that.

Spiral of Awakening and Transformation

A simplified example from one of my many deep layer cake experiences went like this: I hit a point in my career where I was senior, experienced, and savvy. I believed things should be going more smoothly and easily, but they weren't. I noticed that I felt like I was constantly striving and working hard for everything, and it wasn't just at work. I was tired, frustrated, and even a little resentful. As I continued to explore why this would be (one way I did this was to review my feelings through the different ups and downs of my life), I realized that most of my life felt like it was about proving myself. I was a perfectionist, pushing myself and others to get to 100 percent or better all the time. I often second-guessed what I'd accomplished, telling myself, "It could have been better."

I started asking myself what kinds of ideas about me, my place in the world and what I was capable of would create these kinds of behaviors. As I asked myself the questions, things would come to my awareness, like the road was rising up to meet me. I connected to subconscious feelings that I wasn't enough—not smart enough, pretty enough, lovable enough, or powerful enough to have the things I really wanted. I realized that to combat these feelings, I was pushing to make things happen—this was the source of the feelings of always struggling.

> *The higher you go the greater your ablity to fulfill your full potential.*

I was spiritually awake enough to know that struggling is not a gift from the Kingdom of Heaven. We're not here to struggle. So why was struggle what my life appeared to be about? That was the **Wake Up!**—simply stopping long enough to ask if something was out of alignment. My feelings of sadness, frustration and resentment were the catalysts. It can be that simple for you— notice something doesn't feel right in your life, and then look into it. The emphasis is on the *feeling*.

Looking into it in this case meant going into the layer cake of my life to discover where I had taken on the belief that I wasn't enough in the first place. Recall from my story earlier in the book that I grew up hearing things like: "Black people have to work twice as hard to have half as much." and "Anything worth having is worth working hard for." and "Never give up." My interpretations of how these commonly held beliefs related specifically to me, as well as experiences with my parents and others, planted the seeds of my subconscious identification with not being enough. My willingness to go back in time to understand whatever emotional, physical, or mental trauma had caused me to create the false belief, gave me the power to release it. The release is part of the **Shake Up!** Step, which for me, involved several techniques described in the book, as well as consultations with spiritual counselors. As I released the layers of this false idea of myself, I created opportunities to re-align with Divine Truth about who and what I am, and also to re-write the story of that aspect of my life. In this case, I was reclaiming the Truth of being a Divine Being, worthy and deserving of all the Blessings in the Kingdom just because I am, not due to my works, color of my skin, or any other human aspect. I was also claiming the power of a Divine Being to create, which simultaneously meant I was releasing the story I had told myself about not being enough to have the life I wanted.

My new story (the **Make Up!** Step) is that I was born enough, and I always have been. I don't have to work myself into the ground trying to prove that to anyone—or even to myself. In this new story, I acknowledge and honor my inner Divinity with choices to think and behave in ways that deepen my connection to spiritual Truth, and enable my life to be a demonstration of this Truth.

Lastly, the **Take Up!** Step included specific ways to live the story on a daily basis. Some new choices I made specifically relating to the new story of being enough included: 1) keeping a more realistic things-to-do list; 2) letting go of having to be in charge of everything and 3) accepting mistakes and failure without negatively judging and beating myself up. Doesn't that feel sweeter, richer, and more beautiful?!

This is how it works over and over. At the beginning, you'll probably be dealing with more significant issues in your ideas of who you are and how to have what you want. It may take weeks of exploration at the beginning. Over time, as you continue to reapply the **4 Steps** to where you are in the moment, it will get quicker to see connections and make shifts. The more you apply the **Steps**, the more you shift; the more you shift, the easier it becomes to keep the process going. As you continue to experience the awakening and healing that comes from applying the **4 Steps**, the intervals *between* applying them changes. As your inner world shifts, so does your outer experience, giving you new situations that can provide an opportunity for healing, releasing, and experiencing a lighter, higher vibration of you. Live life, feel your feelings, apply the **4 Steps**, and the beat goes on!

In this way, you're never really "done." You are on a constant growth journey—growing into a relationship with yourself, transcending the false aspects of the mighty ego, the false-self, and using your expanded wisdom to claim higher ground. This higher ground is your Higher Consciousness, and the higher you go, the greater your ability to achieve your full potential. You are creating the ability to

Dance Your Soul Lightstyle!

You may come to places in the journey where you feel like you're in a blank spot, which I think of as the Void. This is the place where you're awake to the problems inherent in acting as the old you, and you're aware of why that doesn't feel good or work so well. But the new you isn't fully birthed yet. When I hit this place, I was a bit unsettled. I knew I couldn't go backwards; but I wasn't sure I was moving forward because there wasn't much outward evidence of the changes I was actively making in my Consciousness. At times, this can be more difficult than encountering the subconscious demons you're trying to release. This is where trust and faith come in the most. This is the time to be gentle with yourself. You may want to spend more time alone and in quiet. You must go easy on yourself, and allow the outer world to catch up with your inner changes.

> *Remember, no judgment, no blame, no shame, and no guilt or punishment, for yourself or others.*

Remember, no judgment, no blame, no shame, and no guilt or punishment, for yourself or others. If something's not working, *lovingly* shift it. If people don't "get" what you're doing or why, let go of the need to convince them or be validated by them. Allow them to have their own experience of the newness of you without trying to influence or control their interpretation of it. Remember that the only person you're "doing" this for is you. It only has to be understood by you, accepted by you, blessed by you, embraced by you, loved by *you*.

In fact, you must flow Love to yourself as you experience the progression through the journey. Situations will show up to be healed more than once. Old anger, fear, and false beliefs, like subconsciously thinking of yourself as unlovable or inadequate, surface from time to time in different situations. Choose to be grateful for the opportunity to go higher and deeper, rather than beat yourself up (old judgment energy) for "still having to deal with" certain things. Know that stuck energy may need to be revisited at different levels in order for you to completely detach from what it meant to you in the past. Just allow what comes up to be exactly as it is, re-apply the **4 Steps**, and stay focused on where you are going instead of where you have been.

Most helpful throughout is to choose to make it an adventure, not corrections born out of some crisis. You are not in a crisis.

You are in an ongoing series of Acts of Creation!

Each choice you make for how you will heal and feel, is a choice to create what you want. Each choice you make to forgive and release, is a choice to create what you want. Each choice you make to claim a deeper relationship with the inner **Essence** of you is a choice to create what you want. Each choice you make to be still and balanced is a choice to create what you want. No matter where you are at any given moment on the new map of your happiness, give yourself credit for every step you take. Celebrate even the tiniest milestones, knowing you are already perfect anyway.

Choose progress, rather than perfection. Your ideas of perfection are generally rooted in false beliefs having to do with seeking love and approval. You get to decide what your definition of progress is—be gentle and compassionate while you commit to doing your best in each moment.

I worked with a spiritual teacher who recommended I make commitments to change in 30-day increments. So I would commit to doing a particular practice for 30 days, and then at the end of that time period, I'd recommit. The smaller chunks of time felt more manageable. I've also applied this technique in one week, and even single day increments. Choose what makes it easiest for you to keep going. Remember you are working in service to

> *Remember you are working in service to yourself.*

yourself. Even baby steps along the way are progress. If you fall off the path, get back on as quickly as you can, and celebrate that victory.

The perfection in journeying to your Magnificent Essence is *within* the journey itself.

You don't need to strive to get it "right." Just keep deepening your self-awareness with self-acceptance and self-love in your heart. Laugh heartily and smile often. Dance in your new-found Freedom. Embrace the exquisite nature of the True You in your own state of **Happy to Be ME!**

Once you wake up, you can never really go back to sleep. Once you notice that change is necessary, it's emotionally painful to ignore the need for that change. Once you awaken and claim your True Self spiritually, it's very painful to ignore that aspect of who you are. So use these **4 Steps** to keep yourself spiraling into your full potential and to keep experiencing your highest good.

Here are some key concepts to remember as you integrate and embody the 4 Steps. I've put them in the first-person to make them more empowering for you.

The world is governed by Spiritual Laws that are in operation 24/7/365.

- When I live and play in harmony with these Laws, it's easier to reach my full potential and create a life of happiness, success and fulfillment.

My most important relationship is with my Higher Consciousness within.

- This Divine nature of me, or **Magnificent Essence**, transcends my created ideas of and attachment to personality, identity, and wounds of the ego.

- As I go below the ego's surface interpretations of my memories, beliefs, and experiences, the connection to and alignment with my Essence makes it easier to know my Purpose, what I truly desire, and to reach my full potential.

Wherever I go, there I am.

- I can't run away from my ideas of myself.

- One constant in all my experiences is me.

- How I show up in my life sets the stage for everything else that shows up.

My outer world will always reflect what's going on inside of me.

- A spiritually-aligned inner Self is the foundation for a vibrant *everything*, wherever I go, whatever I do, whoever I'm with.

- When I am spiritually-aligned on the inside, I am a better leader, student, parent, soul mate, and friend in my outer world.

- When I am spiritually-aligned on the inside, a peaceful, effortless and fulfilling life is promised.

If I want to manifest a life of glee,
I have to think, feel, and act from the Highest ME.

Here are some ways to check-in on your **Happy to Be ME!** experience. How many of the statements on the list would you like to be able to claim as how you are feeling and acting? How many are already true for you? From wherever you start, your implementation and embodiment of the **4 Steps** will help you spiral higher.

- I am recognizing myself as a Divine Being, consciously acting in accordance with Universal Laws.

- I am actively engaged in knowing myself deeply, accepting everything about myself, and loving myself unconditionally.

- I have changed my story about who I am and how the world works.

- I am claiming my True Self, and leading my life in alignment with my Higher Consciousness.

- I am feeling Oneness and acknowledging and honoring the Divinity in myself, as well as all beings and things, even if they don't.

- I am quieting my conscious, ego-based mind and listening for my intuitive Soul-based voice.

- I am free from the past and future, anchored in the now moments.

- I act from the energy of the heart, using compassion, tolerance, forgiveness and Unconditional Love as the foundations for everything I say and do.

- I feel lighter inside and I move through life with effortless effort.

- I laugh easily and smile from within often.

- I am a source of light and love for all who come into contact with me.

- My life feels like a series of miracles, unfolding in perfect timing for my highest good.

- I feel a sparkle in my expression and a bounce in my step.

- I am living my purpose; I am also contributing my Divine Light to the planet in selfless service.

- The concepts of self-doubt, fear, lack, limitation, disease, separation, competition, and other low-Consciousness ideas no longer underlay my thoughts, feelings, or actions.

- I fear death less, if at all.

- I am less focused on having security, sensory experiences and power over others.

- I experience problems, disappointments, and delays as powerful opportunities for me to go deeper into the evolution of my Consciousness, and actively look for the guiding messages in each situation.

- I am positive, energized, inspired, and enthusiastic.

- I am filled with gratitude and a profound sense of belonging.

- I feel comfortable in my skin and just being myself is easy and fulfilling.

- *I am Spirit Dancer—leading from my heart, feeling joyful, peaceful and loving through all my experiences, and expecting only good to flow to me.*

Periodically, come back to this list to see how your spiral of transformation is going. Checking-in with them is especially helpful when you hit the places where you perceive that you are stagnating, or you are revisiting the same old energy too many times. You may find that you have spiraled higher than you're giving yourself credit for. Regardless of what you decide, keep going. Keep applying and embodying the **4 Steps**, and you will change your Consciousness and your life!

FREE Your LIGHTSTYLE

Experiment with Ways to Express the Evolving You

Unleash your imagination, dream vividly,
and dance your Soul Lightstyle, expecting
magic and miracles along the way!

CONGRATULATIONS!

You've made it through the 'teachings' part of the book, and there's more. The rest of the book, "Free Your Lightstyle," is designed to help you continue integrating the key spiritual concepts while you also experiment with ways to embody your learnings. The ideas are clustered in distinct sections to make it easier to dance with the ideas in each area. The first section, "You with You," is about how you connect with yourself. Section two, "You and Your Routines," will help you explore what's beneath the surface of your routines and habits. The final section, "You in Your World," supports your exploration of your connection with the world around you.

My suggestion is to skim through all three Sections and see what calls to you. Again, you can try the tips and tools randomly or in any order you choose. You should *not* just default to the order in which they are presented. Connect internally with what has the greatest opportunity for a shift to your Higher Consciousness from where you are now. Listen for your intuitive inner guidance—it should be getting louder since you've been applying the **4 Steps**. If you feel your relationship with yourself needs help, start with that section. Perhaps you feel really locked into your ideas of how you do life. This suggests spending time evaluating your attachment to your routines. You might have uncovered feelings like you somehow don't belong in the world you have been experiencing. It might serve you best to start with the "You in Your World" section.

Wherever you start, remember there are no rights and wrongs, and the experiences you have in each Section are more important than getting finished. As you move from suggestion to suggestion, do your best to stay present and peaceful. No sense of this being a chore or an exercise will support you. Those sentiments are actually a form of resistance. If you feel that way, stop and apply the **4 Steps** to those feelings to see what their message is. Once you are clear, renew your commitment to go through the next sections with enthusiasm and curiosity. Make this phase a part of the birth of your new playfulness.

If you tend to get overwhelmed when you see lots of options on a page, perhaps it would serve you to create a separate notebook in which you can put each individual option as you choose to experience it. That way, you won't have to look at all the options I've given you at once, but you'll still have a place to capture your thoughts and feelings as you play with the ideas.

Finally, I've had powerfully positive awarenesses come from repeating an exercise months or even a year after I started working with the Steps. It has been a wonderful way to give myself ongoing check-ins on my progress. In nearly every case, I've shifted in supportive, enriching, and life-altering ways. Consciously looking for and acknowledging your victories can help you continue to trust in and apply the Steps over time.

Okay, enough with the guidance. It's time for action! Turn the page, and continue your journey into *Dancing Your Soul Lightstyle.*

True Happiness
is to experience
all manner of worldly
sorrow, pain or loss
and still be joyful in
my heart.

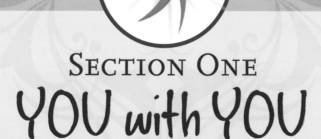

SECTION ONE
YOU with YOU
Getting Clear on How You Relate to Yourself

LOOK FOR THE GIFT HIDDEN IN YOUR STRUGGLE

The only way out is through. ~ Robert Frost

I want to tell you a story about a man and an Emperor moth, the most majestic species among all the moths, with wide and colorfully marked wings. It's a story about gifts, struggle, and life.

One day a man found a cocoon of an Emperor moth. He took it home so that he could watch the moth emerge from its cocoon. He sat and watched the moth as it did what nature had instructed it to do for its birth. Gradually, a little hole appeared in the end of the cocoon, and the moth began to push its way through. As the man watched, he was amazed at the experience of nature in her wonder. He had never seen an Emperor moth emerging into its brilliance. As the process continued, the man started to feel as if the moth was struggling a lot to force its body through the hole in the cocoon.

He watched its efforts for hours and hours. Then the moth seemed to stop making any progress. The body and the cocoon seemed stuck, suspended in time, in a place that the man was sure must be painful to the little moth. Had it really gotten as far as it could go? It just seemed wrong to the man for the struggle to end this way.

Then the man, being kindhearted and compassionate, decided to help the moth. So he took a pair of scissors and snipped at the remaining bit of the cocoon to enable the moth to emerge more easily. When it did, the man noticed it had a swollen body and small, shriveled wings. The freed moth appeared as a fat and shriveled worm-like creature. It was not what he expected at all. He thought for a moment and decided that this must be normal. The wings would eventually enlarge and expand, and the body, now fat and heavy looking, would contract. So he waited.

> The struggles of your life, the heartaches, pains, missteps, and failures, especially as you choose to change, actually are gifts.

To his dismay, neither change happened! In fact, this majestic of all moths, a creature of amazing capability and beauty, spent the rest of its life crawling around with a swollen body and shriveled wings. It never made it to its full splendor and it never got to soar. A few days later, it died.

What the man, in his kindness and haste, did not understand was that the restricting cocoon and the struggle required for the moth to get through the tiny opening, was the way of forcing fluid from the body of the moth into its wings so that it would be ready for flight. Freedom and flight would only come *after* this struggle. By depriving the moth of its struggle, the man had unwittingly deprived the Emperor moth of vitality and life.

You see, the struggles of *your* life, the heartaches, pains, missteps, and failures, *especially as you choose to change*, actually are gifts. They are like the polishing cloth is to the diamond, the water creating grooves in stone. They are the means through which you can move beyond the limiting nature of your lower Consciousness and its ideas about you and the world, into the full potential expression of your **Magnificent Essence.**

Instead of resisting and trying to circumvent your struggles, you'd be better served to go *into* them. You must be willing to open what the ego wants you to believe is a Pandora's Box to see what gems are hidden out of view inside. You'd be better served to go into your pain, rather than try to suppress it or run away from it. You'd be better served by investing energy to get a below-the-surface look at your struggles to understand *why* you're experiencing them. If you can courageously open your heart in love to the aspects of yourself and your life that feel ugly, painful or awful, you can truly heal and transcend them.

The struggles of your life reveal information about your relationship with yourself. What are your struggles trying to show you about how you are stuck, being held back by something inside you that is a part of the false self? How are the mistakes offering you a **Wake Up!** call to remember who you truly are, what you're capable of, and what you came here to do? What are the struggles calling you to choose? How are the disappointments showing you that you need to push the life blood of your **Essence** into your wings so you can soar?

As you greet each one with compassionate curiosity and forgiveness, you make an energetic statement of knowing that you are not meant to struggle. You make a statement of willingness to align with your good. You acknowledge that there is more for you than what is currently showing up. You say "yes" to receiving clarity on how to make things better. You stand up for yourself and create a giant opening to shift your life to a higher vibration. As the Robert Frost quote at the beginning of the story says, to get out of the life you're living, you must go through the life you're living. Continuing to apply the **Steps** will help you go through all aspects of it with more courage and confidence, more awareness, acceptance and Unconditional Love, as well as more ease, Peace and Grace.

Investing in yourself this way is how you create a personal freedom that is exquisite, and like no other. You unshackle yourself from limitations. You release yourself from ego's prison of judgement, lack and fear. You emerge with more peace in your heart, feeling supported in all aspects of your life, and dancing as the powerful Divine Being that you always have been. It's how, in the words of Martin Luther King, Jr., you can exclaim: "Free at last, free at last, thank God Almighty, I am free at last!"

GET CLEAR ON THE MEANING OF YOUR LIFE

In the wake of the September 11, 2001 tragedy at the World Trade Center buildings in New York City, a pair of documentary filmmakers, Jules and Gedeon Naudet, wanted to understand more about the whys underneath the religious conflicts plaguing our world. They began a quest to meet the world's spiritual leaders to ask some very deep and specific questions, and to hear directly from them what the world should know. The adventure culminated in a film and a book entitled *In God's Name: Wisdom from the World's Great Spiritual Leaders.*

Not surprisingly, one of the questions is "What is the meaning of life?" Below, in its entirety, is the response from then Dalai Lama, Tenzin Gyatso, Spiritual Leader of Tibetan Buddhists:

> [The meaning of life is] To be a really peaceful man, conscious, not having fear, if such there be, that is what I think is perhaps the significance of life. There is no joy if we have wealth, but fear in one's mind. So many of us who are attached to the external materials and name, experience fear in mind and live under a great stress. That is why people become old before being old. And they die before the time of death.
>
> The external facilities are no doubt important, but along with that, it is very important to stay peaceful, happy, and conscious. Thinking only about the material development, the external facilities, and not giving attention toward the creation of inner joy, is fulfilling only one out of a pair of the requirements in one's life.
>
> And again, claiming to have inner peace and living deprived of external facility is a sort of another half-life. We have a physical body; we need external material development. But we have a mind, and this mind has different emotions, on the basis of which, we have to inculcate joy and happiness for ourselves. In this context, if we don't

pay attention to the way of inner thinking, our life will be just like a machine; we will be like mechanical people. We have to be peaceful and serene in mind. And the external materials cannot make us joyful in mind. This cannot be purchased by money. This cannot be created by machines."

Notice the call in the Dalai Lama's words—the inner you is the source of true joy and peace. The outer can work in harmony with that, but not instead of it. When there is fear within you, there is no true chance for joy. Prolonged fear and stress create premature death. There must be a balancing of the inner state and the outer expression for life to have meaning. How will you apply the **4 Steps** to achieve this in your life?

The Meaning of *Your* Life

Now, it's *your* turn. It's time to check-in with your heart. What is the meaning of *your* life? How are you living and what legacy are you creating? Are you a prisoner of fear and therefore, creating lack and limitation? Or perhaps your focus on material success has you living a life that is without fulfillment, inner peace, and freedom. What is the meaning of your life?

_____

_____

_____

_____

_____

_____

_____

_____

If you're having trouble answering, here are some suggestions to help you get clarity:

1. Create a list of the things to which you give your greatest attention and focus. The things that we spend the most time and energy on tend to be our reasons for being.

_____

_____

_____

_____

_____

_____

_____

_____

_____

_____

2. Assess the items on the list. Are they there by default (like you've been doing them forever), or are you consciously choosing to do them today? Defaults like your job (store manager, nurse, executive assistant) or your identity (student, athlete, son) are probably not what you want your life to stand for. Lives that have meaning are created from conscious choices nurtured by committed action.

3. For each item, retrace the key decisions that you made and choices you avoided that were the defining moments for why these items are on your list.

_____

_____

_____

_____

_____

_____

_____

_____

_____

_____

4. What values, perceptions, fears, and personality traits most influenced those decisions and avoidances?

_____
_____
_____
_____
_____
_____
_____
_____
_____
_____

5. Star or highlight the things you are willing to change and underline those to which you are attached. What do you notice about them? Can you characterize them a certain way?

_____
_____
_____
_____
_____
_____
_____
_____
_____
_____

With this deeper understanding of you, you are better equipped to ask and answer this critical question: How is what I'm doing and why I'm doing it fulfilling me and giving meaning to my life?

_____

_____

_____

_____

_____

_____

_____

_____

Do your answers add up to lots of fulfillment and meaning? Are you 100 percent comfortable and wanting to keep everything as is? Then Hallelujah! Keep on keeping on! If you are like me when I did this assessment, you ended up with questions and concerns about what you're doing and why. You may even be disappointed with yourself for why you made the choices that got you where you are. Once again, I say Hallelujah! But this time, it's for different reasons.

Hallelujah! that you have awakened to a discontent that you may not have been aware of before. Hallelujah! that you want your life to mean more, inside and out. Until you come to this awareness, you can't change anything. Do not beat yourself up with judgment or disapproval. Don't compare yourself to someone else. Their journey is theirs, just as yours is yours. You are where you are, and you don't need to place a value judgment on it. Let it be perfect, and be grateful for all you have learned from your experiences thus far. Acknowledge all you have contributed to the lives around you.

Because you took time to contemplate the questions and search your heart for some answers, you now have a wonderful opportunity to step into a more glorious experience than ever before—the chance to create the life that will bring you more joy, peace, and abundance!

Yes, precious Soul, you are at a choice point. You can choose to complacently accept the life you're living as your fate, or you can empower yourself to step toward your destiny. Your conscious choices are what can help you have the life you want. The answers to the meaning of your life are inside you. Spending time in quiet contemplation, as well as active engagement in the options that feel right, will help you uncover the hidden desires of your heart.

It's never too late—in fiction or in life—to revise.
~ Nancy Thayer

The following key question can help you get closer to what might hold the key to a life of meaning for you: What am I doing when time seems to stand still, focus is effortless, and I produce joyfully? Describe in detail what this is.

_____

_____

_____

_____

_____

_____

_____

_____

_____

_____

How can you shift more of your time to doing whatever that is? Don't get bogged down trying to figure out how you make money doing it, or whether it can be a career. For now, just see if you can invest even one hour into being that. As you spend more time in the effortless energy of whatever that is, you'll feel even more deeply the wonder and joy in it. Your vibration will go higher. Connections will synchronistically materialize that enable you to explore it even more. Over time, you'll be able to choose how and when to take it to the next level. Or you'll see if something else holds even more of a pull for you.

Be patient and allow yourself the full experience. Dabble in something, ask your inner guidance if it feels right, listen for the answer, and repeat until you know without doubt you've found what it is. At that point, you will feel so inspired and uplifted, you will probably be ready to move mountains to incorporate it in a major way into your life.

This doesn't necessarily mean it will become your new career instantaneously. It might still be a side passion for a while. But even as such, I guarantee, you'll be more happy than you were at the outset, when you discovered the things you were doing brought little meaning to your life. Remember, you have to be willing to do the exploration to find the treasure. It doesn't have to be hard or scary or dark to go inward and ask yourself some questions. It does take courage and determination to complete the journey. Your relationship with yourself, and how you engage yourself relative to consciously choosing your life path are critical to your happiness and success. When you trust that you have the answers within, and you remain open to the Divine wisdom that comes, you chart your course with confidence and freedom.

QUIET YOUR MIGHTY MIND

Meditation is the experience of the limitless nature of the mind when it ceases to be dominated by its usual mental chatter. ~ David Fontana

As you hopefully agree by now, your relationship with you is the place to start your journey to **Living Happy to Be ME!** The voice of your Divine Self can be heard best from a place of inner stillness. The connection to the True you is enhanced when the distraction of "noise" is quieted as you turn within. Meditation is the technique for drawing the attention of the mind inward to experience deeper levels of your own intelligence. It is a way of connecting to the unified field of Oneness at the foundational levels of mind and matter. Meditation is simply an alert, restful state, in which your brain functions with significantly greater ease, and your body gains deep rest.

In the West, many perceive meditation as "woo woo," or religious. Scientific evidence shows it's a concrete practice that impacts the brain and body in significant ways. Meditation stimulates the prefrontal cortex, which is responsible for higher thinking. It also causes the release of naturally-occurring brain chemicals known as neurotransmitters, including dopamine (an anti-depressant), serotonin (associated with increased self-esteem), oxytocin (pleasure hormone whose presence is elevated during sexual arousal), and brain opiates (natural pain killers). These have been linked to different aspects of happiness.

> The voice of your Divine Self can be heard best from a place of inner stillness.

Mind chatter is the number one issue that people complain about when they start on the journey to inner stillness. It's a very real phenomenon. According to various experts, the human brain can consider up to 60,000 thoughts per day! So, in high gear, your brain is wandering through 2,500 thoughts per hour, or roughly 42 thoughts per minute. At these rates, it's no wonder that when your conscious mind is on autopilot or overdrive, you feel stressed, contracted, and out of sorts.

Now, think about the mind more holistically and go beyond the head's mind chatter. The True Mind is an integration of conscious mind (head) and subconscious mind (heart). When I *hear* the chatter in my head, I also *feel* a sensation associated with it somewhere else in my body. When my conscious mind is swept up in thoughts of fear about money or survival, I not only hear the words of a fearful story or question going through my head, I also feel a stirring in my solar plexus, a constriction in my heart, and sometimes tears welling up in my eyes. I'll venture a guess that you, too, can identify body sensations associated with certain "stressful" thoughts.

Your whole physiological system can go into a quasi-fight or flight mode as you try to manage the internal stress caused by this combination effect of "mind chatter." Importantly, mind chatter doesn't really cease. It's a natural by-product of the conscious mind being the conscious mind. It's important to accept that for most of us, some level of that inner noise is pretty much here to stay.

Your greatest opportunity for staying connected to your **Magnificent Essence** within is to recondition yourself such that the *impact* of the chatter can be diminished over time, allowing you to rest and recharge inside. This is the center of the idea of "quieting the mind," as I have experienced and referenced it.

In "The Journey Inward," blogger, Schweta, writes beautifully about the experience of quieting thoughts. Paraphrasing from one of her posts, here is an explanation:

> Before creating a meditation practice, constant mind chatter can make you feel like the mind has 100 acres of space, and it's 100 percent chatter. It is a constricted space constantly filled with thoughts. When you start meditation, there is an immediate shift. The total acreage of the mind appears to expand to maybe 200 acres. But now, the thought-consumed acreage feels like it's only 50 percent of the

total mind. So there are now 100 acres of thoughts and 100 acres of silence. As you continue developing your meditation practice, you experience your mind as vast acreage, but only a portion cultivating thoughts. Imagine over time, you experience the mind as 100,000 acres of silence and still just 100 acres of thoughts. The 100 acres of thoughts stay there always, that is what the mind does. But the silence increases and so the thoughts seem like a tiny spec in that vast silence.

Another goal is to be *awake* enough in your life to catch the *nature* of the chatter. What is the story underneath it? What is the emotional hook attached to it? What is the chatter saying about who you believe you are in the world? The quality of your thoughts should be as much a focus as the quantity of them. Thoughts that are negative, like those that created fear and sadness in me, hurt you in the short- and long-term. They cause disruption in sleep, increase stress levels, trigger reactions, and keep you running, chasing after outcomes that make you "feel better."

> You may be completely on autopilot, sleepwalking through your experiences without consciously choosing your responses in the moment.

As you go through the **Happy to Be ME! 4 Step** process, and explore the many exercises in this "Free Your Lightstyle" part of the book, you will get clarity on what's underneath your mind's chatter. Remember that you have been conditioned to think a certain way, believe certain things, and behave accordingly. This conditioning started at a very young age and has continued throughout your life. You may be completely on autopilot, sleepwalking through your experiences without consciously choosing your responses in the moment. Your mind chatter is part of that conditioned response to what's going on around you, and you may be telling yourself the story that you can't do anything about it. "It just happens and I can't turn it off!" people often exclaim to me.

I know it can *seem* that way, but you really can recondition your responses to every situation and create a quieter mind. Meditation is one of the firmest foundations for me in this aspect of my personal journey. The stillness of meditation is a place of rest and rejuvenation, as well as the way to stay connected

to the **Magnificent Essence** within. Meditation gives me an opportunity to disconnect from the go-go-do-do world around me, and be motionless. Meditation can be that for you as well. You simply have to make the choice that it is something you will incorporate into your experience, commit to establish the schedule and practice that works for you, and take ongoing action to joyfully create the habit.

I love both silent meditation and guided meditation, and I actively practice at least once just about every day. I use 1-2 minute refreshers in the midst of what looks like chaos going on around me, and routinely use 30-60 minute sessions as my foundation.

I'm a practitioner of Transcendental Meditation (TM) from the Vedic tradition of enlightenment in India. TM has been handed down through Vedic masters for thousands of years, and today is practiced by millions of people from various cultures and walks of life. If fact, TM is considered one of the most popular meditation techniques in the world.

TM is also the most widely researched of all meditation techniques. Over 600 research studies have been conducted at more than 250 universities and research centers (including Harvard, UCLA, and Stanford), resulting in hundreds of published reports of benefits from the practice of TM.

It's a simple practice requiring 20 minutes of quiet time, twice per day, while seated comfortably. It is a very specific practice however, and the same procedures have been transferred from gurus to practitioners very carefully to ensure maximum effectiveness.

Many other forms of meditation are acknowledged worldwide including, vipassana meditation, Zen meditation, Taoist meditation, mindfulness meditation, and Buddhist meditation. Some forms require the body to be still and others, like Japa meditation, allow for doing other activities while doing the meditation.

Regardless of the methods, the purpose is universal: quiet the mind, release stress and anxiety, and connect with the inner field of wisdom. There is easily enough content to write a separate book on meditation, and since many exist already, for the purpose of deepening your connection with you, suffice it to say this is a critical component of the action plan.

Meditation is a profound experience for millions from all walks of life around the world. But many people hear the word "meditation" and they react in fear or frustration. First, they may have ideas about how difficult it might be to meditate. They may have told themselves they need training and they don't have a guru. Maybe they've tried to meditate on their own and they feel like it didn't "work" or they didn't do it "right." Maybe they can't imagine getting into a lotus position, let alone holding it for 20 or 30 minutes, while they empty their minds of all thought. And that last one, "emptying the mind of all thought," probably creates the biggest barrier.

Hopefully none of these things are true for you. There's no need for all that negative energy rattling around inside you. Meditation offers such amazing benefits that it is worth breaking down any barriers to incorporating it into your life. If you are feeling stressed and chronically tired, or you sometimes lack clarity or creativity, meditation can help. If emotional reactions are making your relationships tiring or difficult, or you're juggling too many to-do's and managing multiple challenges, meditation can help.

The world can be fast-paced, demanding, and disappointing. Over time, dealing with all of this raises stress levels, lowers immunity, and increases worry, fear, and fatigue. It's no surprise that millions are struggling to keep up, and finding it hard to feel peaceful, empowered, and happy in the process.

Meditation is a free, 100 percent accessible, and portable solution! You don't need a doctor's referral, and no expensive pills or equipment are necessary. Just get quiet, turn within, and you're on your way to experiencing the many benefits that routine meditation has to offer, including:

- ♥ More peacefulness

- ♥ Reduced stress

- ♥ Increased immunity

- ♥ Lowered blood pressure

- ♥ Increased oxygen to the brain (which enhances creativity and problem-solving ability)

Once you get started reaping the rewards of routine meditation, you may wonder how you managed for so long without it! You will eventually crave the stillness. I know I do! Why not get started today?!

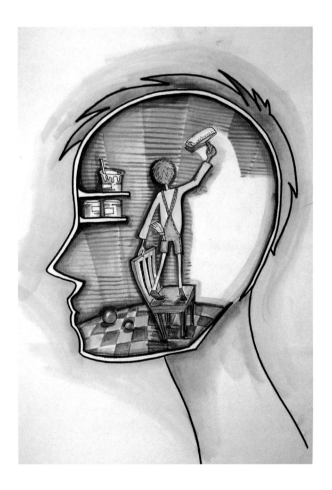

TAKE A STAND FOR SELFISHNESS

I am resolved to be more selfish, and I'm inviting you to join me! "Why on earth would I want to do that?" you ask. Because even a little self-awareness, self-care, self-respect, and self-love—what I call healthy and responsible selfishness—can bring a lot of powerfully positive experiences into your life! Of course, I'm talking about capital S selfishness, as in: tuning into and being in relationship with your higher Self.

I have taught marketing at The Paul Merage School of Business at the University of California, Irvine, on a part-time basis since 2007. On many occasions, I also bring my life-mastery principles into discussions, especially when personal leadership is involved. In one lecture with two different groups of nearly 100 students each, I waded into new territory. I shared my perspective on what it takes to be a successful leader in a 90-minute talk entitled, "Leadership for Success." My focus is on an area of leadership that I believe is not widely or deeply taught.

After asking the students to share what they believed were the "hallmarks" of their personal leadership styles, I discovered one foundational aspect completely missing: a deep relationship with and continual care of self. When I asked why no one had included "relationship with self" or "self-realization," or "self-care," or some other term that reflects knowing and expressing from the higher Self, what I heard was disappointing, albeit, not surprising.

The students were concerned that this kind of focus would make them selfish leaders. While communication, negotiation, collaboration, listening, engaging, and motivating were seen as imperative, among other things, focus on one's self is not regarded as a key trait for world-class leadership. In fact, I'd struck a nerve—they were intrigued with how boldly I was taking a stand for selfishness, something just about all of them had learned was downright unacceptable in most aspects of life.

Without a doubt, the various definitions of the word selfish make it clear that to be so is not good. However, the negativity feels driven by the aspects of the definitions that make the behavior ego-based and exclusive—a 24/7/365 focus on self.

I've emphasized such language in the following definitions to make my point. For example, the Encarta Dictionary defines selfish as "Looking after one's own desires; concerned with your own interests, needs, and wishes *while ignoring those of others*." It defines selfishness as "the condition of habitually putting one's own interests before those of others." The World English Dictionary defines selfish as "Chiefly concerned with one's own interest, advantage, etc, especially to the *total exclusion of the interests of others*." Dictionary.com says: "1. Devoted to or caring *only* for oneself; concerned primarily with one's own interests, benefits, welfare, etc., *regardless of others*; 2. characterized by or manifesting concern or care *only* for oneself."

I will agree, focus on self to the exclusion of all else all the time, is neither healthy nor appropriate. But when you strip out the lingo of exclusivity and look deeper at the rest, the definitions provide guidance for exactly what I believe is a foundation for a happy and vibrant life—an exploration and valuing of inner interests and welfare, which feel both healthy and responsible. Here's my own definition of the kind of inner focus I'm calling for:

> *Basing my choices on my needs, desires, and welfare without losing compassion for and interest in others; ensuring that I know and value my True Self.*

There's no "only" or "to the exclusion of" or "regardless of." I'm not saying that I stop caring *about* or *for* others. Nor do I suggest *my* interests be the focus for others in my world. I'm not saying you should focus on me, take care of me, make me happy, or treat me as the centerpiece of your life. In fact, those actions are more about codependency, and they have no place in a model for vibrant living. I am simply suggesting that all our relationships, our ability to create our own happiness, our connection to our passion, and our ability to express truth are all enhanced by how well we connect to our deepest and most truthful Self. This is the centerpiece of how I take the best care of me. It's how I connect best to the peace, love, abundance, and freedom that is my birthright.

The negative view of selfishness is learned behavior. In fact, I learned it just like the students who brought it up during my talk. It started for me at home, where we were taught that we had specific and important responsibilities to the family and to the smooth running of the household. This included watching out for each other on the walk to school, helping with homework, and of course, chores, like washing dishes and keeping our rooms in order. Then came Girl Scouts, sports teams, school clubs, church leadership, which all have cultures focused on service

to others. Add to that, popular culture with famous lines like "The needs of the many outweigh the needs of the few." (Mr. Spock in *Star Trek: The Wrath of Khan*) and away we go.

It's no wonder you are so outwardly focused! But here's the problem—when you're talking about creating a vibrant life, living your purpose, following your passion, being successful, feeling peaceful, feeling happiness—being focused so much on the needs of others, while ignoring your own, can create situations ranging from uncomfortable to disastrous. It may not be such a big deal if you end up going to a movie you never wanted to see or eating a meal you wouldn't choose, just to please your date once in a while. These can be a part of the natural give-and-take in relationships.

But, it goes deeper than that. I was amazed at how many students in my talks admit to pursuing a college major solely because it will please their parents, even though they have little or no interest in the discipline. That is a personal sacrifice of several years! Do you know anyone doing work they don't like because they are afraid their spouse won't condone what they really want to do? Ever hear someone lament not pursuing a dream because their family would think they were crazy? How many parents in unhealthy relationships are staying together solely for the children's sake? I talk to countless people who don't really know how to find their purpose and passion, or who are uncomfortable being alone.

I would suggest that making selfishness bad or undesirable on the surface doesn't serve us. My healthy and responsible version of Selfish just means making a choice about what comes *first*. It's about ensuring *my* needs and desires fit into the equation of *my* life. It reminds me of the pre-departure safety demonstration on airplanes. We're told that if the oxygen masks drop down from the overhead compartment, we should put our own mask on first, before helping someone else with theirs. I take this to mean that being hero/heroine for those around us requires us to be a hero/heroine to ourselves first.

Yet, I know many people who've sacrificed so much of themselves to their work, their parents, their children, the PTA, the soccer team, the alumni association, and on and on. They are totally disconnected from being that hero for themselves. That's a real shame, and if this is you, I invite and encourage you to shift. Remember the **Make Up!** Step. Think of your life as your very own big budget feature film. As you write and produce the next chapter of your life epic about happiness, fulfillment and success, don't cast yourself as an extra when you should really be the star! And keep in mind...there is only one performance. You don't get to rehearse. This is it.

As you work with the **4 Steps** to take a look at your life and how you're living it, remember to ask yourself: Is the way I treat myself an asset? Do my choices enrich me, attract goodness, and make my life feel expansive? Am I choosing people, places and things that nurture and support me, keeping me healthy, peaceful, and happy? Am I breathing new life into my life? Am I getting beyond my personality and identity to get to the deepest aspects of my Higher Self, and letting my **Magnificent Essence** lead?

Or am I my own worst enemy? Seeing things only through the wounds, biases and separation of the ego. Am I living in my past, worried too much about pleasing others, or afraid to express my brilliance because others might take offense? Am I feeling unfulfilled, but not changing things so I don't rock the boat? Am I locked in a downward spiral of discontent? Am I accepting what doesn't please me because I don't know what will?

I started off this section with the phrase "I am resolved to be more selfish." By rearranging some of the letters, out of that comes the affirmation: "I love Self more." How about it? Are you ready to shift into a deeper relationship with your Self? Start by getting clear on the choices you're making. Perhaps you'll see that some healthy and responsible Selfishness would be the start to a life you love living. Everything in life is choice. That's what free will is about. If you're not choosing you, who are you choosing and why?

LET PLEASURE REIGN SUPREME

How often do you do things simply for the pleasure of it? Not to learn something, or advance your career, or connect with like-minded people, or contribute to the well-being of the planet, or to make a positive impression. Not for any reason at all, except so that *you* enjoy the experience. How often? For many of us, it can be all too rare! Yet, there's at least one really good reason to engage in just-for-the-pleasure-of-it experiences as often as possible. It's about raising your energetic vibration, which can change ... everything. This simple inner awareness is what underlies the Law of Attraction.

Vibrational energy exists in and all around us. Simplistically speaking, the vibrational pull between particles, or how fast the energy molecules spin, dictates how they form into one thing or another. The energy particles making up a chair are spinning at a different rate (have a different pull or attractive power) than those particles that make up you. You can't access this vibrational activity with your five senses, so it's not surprising that most people aren't tuned-in to the energetic aspect of how the world works, or the power it holds in our lives. Consider this part of your **Wake Up!** call to get clear on the energetic Truth of who you are.

You see, it's this vibrational pull and *not* what we say or think that really lies at the center of our power of attraction. I like to say *"As ye vibrate, so shall ye receive."* This means that the energetic vibration or pulse of you is more powerful than the intellectual aspects of you. Take a deep breath and allow that to really land. We talked in the **Shake Up!** Step about the iceberg below the surface—the subconscious layer of you. What's going on at that level—

> The heart's electrical field is about 60 times greater in amplitude than the electrical activity generated by the brain.

what I call the "heart vibe"—is more powerful than the knowledge and intellect of the conscious mind. Getting this idea fully can make a world of difference in your peace, prosperity, abundance, and happiness.

The intuitive power of the heart has been studied by the Institute of HeartMath (IHM) for over 2 decades. I love IHM and all it's contributing to head-heart integration and personal healing. IHM's research is prolific and quite amazing. Two IHM studies looked at the heart's energetic communication, or "cardioelectromagnetic communication." According to IHMs findings, "the heart's electrical field is about 60 times greater in amplitude than the electrical activity generated by the brain." This makes the heart the most powerful generator of vibrational energy in your body. This field can be measured by electrocardiogram and detected on your skin. Here's the kicker: the heart's magnetic field is "more than 5,000 times greater in strength than the field generated by the brain." So what's going on in your heart—how you *feel* about yourself and situations around you—will influence what you attract more than your thoughts.

This is why it's imperative to know what's influencing your heart vibes. As you have traversed the hills and valleys, deserts and oases in your life, you've picked up beliefs, values, and perceptions, and gotten stuck in emotions that don't serve you. Using the **Shake Up!** tools, you can do careful inward review, and uncover the incidences that happened when you were a child that are still influencing your heart vibe. Whether these are fears about lack and limitation, sadness and hurt about feeling inadequate or unworthy, shame or guilt from some past mistake or "failure," it doesn't really matter. What's important is to know that whatever low-vibration emotion you are energetically sending out, it will attract its like in your outer experience.

Yes, the vibrational pull of those embedded energetic fragments dictate what you attract, much *more* than your affirmative intentions, your dream book and vision board, or your goal statements and action plans. If you want to attract more of the things you consciously want, you must take action to raise your energetic vibration. The release work of the **Shake Up!** Step is critical.

Doing things simply for the pleasure of it will also help. When you want to boost your energetic vibration, you can add things to your experience that open your heart, make you laugh, allow you to be playful and free, give you comfort, alleviate stress, or help you get more sleep. When you combine an increase in pleasurable experiences, especially without needing to get anything more out of them, you can activate the joy within your State of Being. The more joy vibration in you, the better.

Now, this is not a license to do anything. Obviously, there are healthy and enriching ways to give yourself pleasure, and other ways that are less healthy, or totally *unhealthy* means of doing so. Choose lovingly, using your inner wisdom as your guide and you'll land on the right thing.

Some examples include a long walk in nature, a nap on a busy day, a comedy show, finger painting or other art, pleasure reading, laughter yoga, a good workout, a guided meditation, a swim in the ocean or a lake, a foot massage, a bubble bath, an hour with your favorite poetry or music—the list is only limited by your creativity and commitment. You get to choose what is just right for you.

One helpful tip is to base this choice and focus this experience *totally on you*. Including someone else can actually add stress, as you compromise to find the one-size-fits-all experience. In the end, your attempt to give yourself a boost might just bring you down further. Also remember, this is not a silver bullet remedy for all that ails you. In most cases, you will need to go deeper into your relationship with yourself to overcome the challenges you face, and find your way to authentic and lasting happiness. Nonetheless, every step counts and every action taken is a meaningful investment in **Living Happy to Be ME!**

How about getting started right now?! On the next page list ten *just-for-the-pleasure-of-it* things you'd like to do *just for you*. Commit to doing them in the next 30 days, and put the dates on the calendar to help you plan for them in advance. Then sign the commitment. If necessary, give a copy of your commitment to an accountability partner and empower them to remind you to fulfill your commitment to yourself.

Have Fun!

I Deserve Pleasure and Fun, Just Because!

My Just-for-the-Pleasure-of-it Wish List	I will gift this to myself on...

I, _____, do hereby commit to gifting myself the above pleasurable activities to help raise my vibration, activate inner joy, and help me feel more happiness. I will do all the activities within the next 30 days, which is by _____.

_____
Signature

_____
My Accountability Partner

Deepen Your Connection to You

If you're like most people, you have a decidedly external focus. This means your list of priorities is a mile wide and 10 miles deep, BUT you're generally not on it. If you're lucky, you *sometimes* make the list, and even then, you are most often at the bottom. It may also mean that you're not as clear on all the aspects of you that there really are. This is an opportunity to catapult yourself to the top of the list and deepen your connection to your inner voice. Engage in the discovery of the "You-Ness" of you.

♥ Spend 30-minutes writing about the qualities of yourself that you believe make you lovable. Over time, expand this to a practice that you engage in at least once a month. Focus on your innate qualities, the things you can't really change, and not your accomplishments.

♥ Watch your favorite movie or read your favorite book again, as if for the first time. Pay attention to how your reactions may have shifted. Is your appreciation more or less than it used to be? Connect with what about you is different and how that difference came about. How might the shift be a clue to something deeper that might need your attention and release?

♥ Spend 5-15 minutes a day for seven days straight looking at yourself in the mirror. Do your best to hold your own gaze. Do not engage with anything else but you. Start with just your face, and over time, expand this to include gazing at your naked body from multiple angles. Note your feelings and your mental chatter. What are they telling you about your relationship with yourself? Where did those feelings/thoughts originate? Do they serve you? Is it your voice speaking them or someone else's? What needs to be healed and released?

♥ Ask 10 friends/family members/colleagues to share in writing what they believe you do well. Tell them to think broadly about you in all your roles. While you're waiting to receive their lists, write your own. See how many things you can come up with. Review their lists and see what surprises you find. How many of the things you captured were on their lists? What *didn't* make the list that also surprises you? Is your external persona matching up to your idea of who you are? Are you acknowledging your gifts or missing them?

♥ Free your inner child. Reconnect with what you used to love to do as a child by doing it as an adult: finger paint, work with clay or Play-Doh, color, sing kid's songs, play in a playground, dance in the rain, fly a kite, hold a finger puppet show, climb a tree, search for seashells at the shore, watch an animated kid's movie, wear bright colors or unmatched socks. Go to a local fair or festival, play games and eat junk food. Buy yourself some balloons! Invite your friends over for a game of Twister and see how much you can laugh. The idea is to awaken the innocence and abandon of your more youthful self to experience the joy and awe that go along with it. Commit to finding ways to keep this aspect of you alive, even though you're living as an adult.

♥ Take an essential oil class and find out how they can help deepen the connection within and/or open you to a different experience of the world around you. What kind of oils do you like best; what uplifts and inspires you?

♥ Do some personal inventories to see if there are patterns that can tell you more about yourself. For example, what genre of books do you enjoy reading the most? Why is that? What colors are most prominent in your wardrobe? Why is that? What kinds of foods do you eat the most and why? What things do you steer clear of and why?

♥ Observe yourself in fearful or risky situations. For example, how do you feel walking up to a stranger to pay them a compliment or ask them a question? How do you feel when a homeless person is near you? How do you engage with really happy or really sad people? Do you avoid eye contact when you're passing people on the street or in the hall? Why or why not? Write down the feelings as you experience them and see what they are telling you about you that might need to be healed or shifted. To what beliefs or past experiences are the feelings linked. Should they be?

PLAY *Write*
DANCE
Move EXPRESS
Create
wonder

Doodle Page

My circumstances reveal the current me. Tapping into the **Magnificent Essence** of me takes me to where I want to be.

Expand Your Expression of the "You-Ness" of You

Ever feel like you're in a personal expression rut? You might notice things like styling your hair the exact same way, or wearing the same "favorites" in your wardrobe, or doing the same kind of vacation year in and year out. Your self-expression is a very personal and unique way you share your **Magnificent Essence** with the world. There is no other being like you.

As you deepen your understanding of and relationship with yourself, you may feel called to express the "You-Ness" of you differently. Go ahead! Explore what feels right, better, best with everything you do to express your inner masculine/feminine, playfulness, youthfulness, wisdom, creativity, joy, and power. Change as often as it feels good to do so. Make it fun and remember, it's personal—you don't have to please anyone but yourself!

- ♥ Find an ethnic grocery store and choose something completely new and different to cook. Experiment and surprise your taste buds! Invite some friends over and share your new experience with them.

- ♥ Tell your hairstylist or barber what's changed with your inner self and ask him/her to help you reflect that on the outer through your hairstyle. See what changes they suggest for your hair and choose one that makes you feel good.

- ♥ Visit the cosmetics or skincare department in an upscale department store and get a make-over or facial. Let the design artist or aesthetician show you how to bring out your best features and match that with your new experience of self.

- ♥ Take up a new hobby that allows personal expression. The options are practically endless. You could take up: a musical instrument, woodworking, drawing or painting, flower arranging, improv comedy or dramatic acting, singing with a choir or solo, photography, or doing handicrafts. You could also join a club that allows you to do the activity with others, which can be even more fun and expansive.

♥ Make edible gifts and personally deliver them to share the new you.

♥ Get out and play a new sport. Many cities have indoor and outdoor facilities for various sports, and leagues you can join that range from beginner to advanced. You might like martial arts, sailing, boxing, horseback riding, rowing, flag football, racquetball or tennis, or one of many other options.

♥ Learn to dance. Explore tango, foxtrot, samba, salsa, two-step, hop-hop, ballet, square or line dancing classes. See if you can find a class that ends with a student performance. Put yourself out there being this new expression of your creative energy and flow.

♥ Learn about a foreign language and culture and use that as the basis for your self-expression. What colors and styles will you wear? What will you eat? How will you walk? How does your external expression change as you incorporate elements of culture and language?

♥ Re-orient your living space. Maybe there are items you love and want to keep forever, so move them to a different place in the room or another room in the house. Weed out the clutter and donate the excess to the community. Take a Feng Shui class and see how you can make your environment an energetically and spiritually supportive sanctuary.

♥ Volunteer in the community where you can contribute your creativity to help others. Maybe a food bank needs help making banners for its next canned food drive. Perhaps the Boys & Girls Club needs people to help make presentations to local businesses, or Habitat for Humanity needs help with painting new houses. Marrying your creative expression with giving to the community is a fabulous way to shine your light on others.

As long as you live, keep learning how to live.

~ Seneca, c. 4 BC-65 AD, Roman Dramatist, Poet

Doodle Page

Inside-out living is going from gut to glory!

_____

_____

_____

_____

_____

_____

_____

_____

_____

_____

_____

_____

_____

_____

_____

_____

_____

_____

_____

_____

_____

_____

_____

Explore the Subconscious You

One of the most important things we need to know is what lies underneath the surface of who we claim to be. Without this understanding, you may be acting out beliefs, values, and interpretations that you don't really want to be expressing. For example, if you're carrying age-old hurts, they may be the source of subconscious fear that is holding you back. If you have hidden resentments or stored anger, you may be causing physical ailments that you're not even aware of yet.

It's important that you take time to discover the parts of you that are not conscious expressions. Otherwise, these blind spots could be creating huge and ongoing problems that you'll never be free of. This section is calling you into a deep exploration. Allow yourself the maximum time to invest yourself in each activity. Note: Exploring deep subconscious blocks may be done best with the support of a coach or spiritual director. Get the help you need to go the furthest on this journey.

- ♥ Work with a spiritual counselor or other coach to take a personal inventory of the peaks and valleys in your life. Connect with what was going on then, how you feel about those situations now, what remnants of the feelings may still remain, what you've learned, etc.

- ♥ Explore your ability to forgive. What blame and resentments are you still holding onto about other people in your life? How many guilts and shames are you hanging onto about yourself? Why? Explore what you're getting from them and decide whether you're ready to let them go. If not now, when?

- ♥ Take a "dormant gift" inventory. What things are you really good at, without working hard, that you haven't nurtured? Why not? Decide if you should change that or not.

- ♥ Gift yourself a 3-day (or longer) silent meditation retreat. See what comes to you from your inner self as you retreat there for several days. How do you receive the silence? Is it peaceful or stressful? What messages are wanting to be heard and understood in a retreat from the noise of your usual day-to-day? Can you receive them?

♥ Explore your fears. What makes you afraid, and where does it come from? Where do you feel the fear in your body? Can you tell how the fear is holding you back or minimizing your presence in your life? Create a "What If" door into your life and assess what your life would be like if you let go of the fears and stepped through it. Make the changes necessary to have the scenario you want.

♥ Notice and keep track of how and when you alter who you are to make others feel good. When do you withhold yourself (stop yourself from saying or doing something you want to say or do)? When do you go along with other people's ideas and desires despite feeling that you don't really want to? What is causing you to do that? What happens in the end when you alter yourself in these ways? What is your real Truth in these moments? What price are you paying for abandoning it?

♥ There's never anything missing from inside any of us. Are you feeling like if you were just more of this or less of that, you'd be enough? What masks are you wearing to fit in better or feel like you're enough? Do a collage of pictures and words to capture the things that come up for you as you contemplate this question. Explore how life would be for you if you stopped wearing the masks. Explore who sees/feels your masks and how they are impacted when you're hiding behind them.

♥ Belief systems can be born inside us at a young age. How far back can you trace your most prominent beliefs about yourself and your place in the world? Create a timeline that traces your ten most Sacred Cow beliefs. How have they served you in the past? Are they still serving you? How are they getting in your way? Which ones are you ready to release?

♥ You have to *integrate* the emotional, intuitive, sacred wisdom of the heart *with* the analytical, intellectual, rational wisdom of the head. How often do you discount your heart's message in favor of your head? Trace a few of the times, looking at the situation and the short-term and long-term outcomes. Is your choice to ignore your heart serving you? How can you quiet the head in similar circumstances and trust your heart more and more?

This moment is
all there is.
~ Rumi

Doodle Page

Doodle Page

All religions, all this singing, is one song. The differences are just illusion and vanity.

~ Rumi

Get Clear on Who You are to You

How do you treat yourself? Are you a nurturing, giving, advocate and friend? Or are you judge, jury, warden, and executioner? I found through various exercises in this section, that I was really hard on myself at deep levels. No matter how successful I became, how beautiful people told me I was, or how many accomplishments I racked up, I still found a way to diminish myself. I had a measuring stick that kept me always in the "not enough" category, and I had harsh punishments for falling short. What a waste. It's imperative that you get real clear on your connection to and relationship with you. Then make a personal commitment to become more loving and kind to yourself.

- ♥ For an entire day, capture and assess your internal voice. Write down the things you say to yourself in every circumstance throughout the day. Whose voice are you hearing? Is the voice saying things you want to be telling yourself or thinking about? If it's not, explore what could be below the surface of the messages. What is coming up that it's time to release? How would your internal voice become more loving and nurturing? How can you ensure you are more positive and supportive with your thoughts?

- ♥ Give yourself a day without self-judgment. Don't make yourself the brunt of any jokes you tell, don't make comments internally or aloud that take issue with anything you do, say, or wear. This doesn't mean you have to gush compliments on yourself. If all you can be is neutral, be neutral. How does that feel inside? Do the situations of the day feel different in any way? Capture your feelings and experiences over a few days and see what you learn.

- ♥ Spend a day completely in solitude. Turn off all connection to the outside world and simply be with you. Notice what comes up for you. Are you fighting the "need' to call someone, or watch TV or get online? Are you having trouble deciding what will make you most happy in the moment? Do you find yourself uninteresting? Do you get bored? Capture your feelings and experiences. What are you noticing about how you feel about yourself? What needs to be healed?

♥ Indulge yourself one way each day for a week (preferably not with food or beverages). Do you believe you're *worth* fresh flowers? Do you feel guilty if you devote time to a luxurious bubble bath (with candles, soft music, and essential oils) or if you break away for a nap? What feelings come up when you want to take a day off from work? Do you feel like it can only be in certain circumstances, or can you not work so you can do nothing? Do you balk at doing things for yourself that you'd easily do for your lover or kids?

♥ Journal on the following question: In what ways are you taking a backseat in your life by working to please others, making your life about being responsible for others, or sacrificing your needs or desires to receive love and happiness from others? What stories are you telling yourself about what would happen if you put yourself first?

♥ Write yourself a love letter. Gush with your affection and gratitude for yourself. Be sure it's simply about the inherent aspects of you, and not your accomplishments. How does it feel to put your love for yourself into concrete words on a page? Let a couple days go by, then read the letter, first silently, then aloud. How does it feel to read your concrete expression of your love for yourself? Are things missing you would like to be more loving toward? Is that something you really don't love or are you expressing feelings about you that you experienced coming from someone else? What are you learning about your relationship with yourself from this experience?

If I want to achieve my highest good,
I have to think, feel, and act from my highest Self.

Practice Capturing Yourself in the Moment

What are you *thinking*?

How are you *feeling*?

YOU and YOUR ROUTINES

Making Conscious Choices in Your Day-to-Day

NOTICE WHAT YOU NOTICE

The joy of creating a vibrant life, the kind of life you desire, is that you are in the driver's seat. You get to decide what "vibrant" means to you, how you go after it, and when you've attained it. Have no doubt that it's possible. I believe you're already fully equipped to create that life right now. In fact, you may already have quite an amazing life and just not be fully aware of it.

How is that possible? How could you not realize the totality or fullness of your life? It depends on what you notice. What is getting your attention, captivating you, holding your focus? Have you got a clear sense in your heart about what is good and great and stupendous in your life? Or are you mired in the muck; anxious about what tomorrow will bring and sleepless with worry about the things going "wrong" that you can't control?

What you notice can really do you good... or do you in. For example, are you noticing the horrible traffic or the number of green lights you slide easily through? Are you totally focused on the team members who are not doing enough, or praising and thanking the ones who contribute? Are you ranting about the professor who doesn't get you, or grateful for the ones who do? Are you still carrying a negative charge about the server in the restaurant who gave you mediocre service, or are you grateful for the hundreds of times the service was exceptional? Did you notice the breeze, a full blossom of new rose, a bunny munching along the trail you walk, or a hummingbird dancing in your garden? And if just now, all you could think was, "I don't have a garden," this message is especially for you because you're noticing things that just don't serve you to reach your highest potential.

Every time you give energy to what you *don't* want, every time you lament, moan, and groan about the things that *don't* work for you—the people who let you down, the food that tasted bad, the boss who doesn't "get" you—every time you emotionally charge that stuff and then keep your attention there, you are asking for more of the same. It's like tuning your radio to an AM station and waiting for your favorite FM station to start playing. It won't happen. It can't happen. They're on different frequencies.

<blockquote>

I am unmoved by appearances and therefore appearances move.

~ Dr. John Kappas
</blockquote>

One of my most favorite mentors had me adopt this affirmation as a reminder to keep my internal vibration neutral and detached, no matter what I was experiencing in my environment at a given moment in time. This neutrality enabled me to be free of emotionally-charged *negative* thoughts and feelings so I could fill myself up with emotionally-charged *positive* thoughts and feelings.

Remember our discussion about Universal Spiritual Laws and the energy dynamics of the Universe? If you want to create more of the things you want, focus your emotional attention and intention on those things, and those things only. Tune the vibrational energy that you emit to the vibrational energy of the good you seek. Release the need to weigh, judge, and condemn the people and situations in your world. Allow what is, to be what it is, and stay centered in the wisdom that a higher power is at work on a plane that isn't necessarily visible or intellectually understandable from your vantage point.

To notice more about what you notice, check-in with yourself frequently on how you're experiencing your life moment-by-moment. Use the table below to start taking inventory of what you give your attention and energy to. What are you noticing? How are you interpreting the situation? What's driving both? The column that's the most full can tell you a lot about your vibration. Once is generally not enough for this exercise, so do it, awaken to your choices, then do it again in 6 months, and see which column is the most full at different points in time.

Date	Good	Great	Stupendous	Something to Complain About

You may not be able to change what is showing up in the outer world in a given moment. But you always, always, *always*, have control over how you react. You have control over how you interpret and engage each situation that you encounter. Always choose feelings and thoughts which serve you by keeping your vibration high, and help you spiral up into your highest good—no matter what outer appearances suggest.

Get Clear on What's Running You

We've explored throughout the book what lies beneath the surface. As you contemplate this section on routines, it's more of the same. You must look at *why* your routine behaviors are your routine behaviors before you can start to consider if and how you want to change them. Are you pushing to make things happen in your life right now? Why? Are you feeling backed up against a wall? Why, and what's "the wall" for you? Time, money, a relationship? It can be practically impossible to find your peaceful center when you feel you have to try so hard to make things happen. So, as the title asks, what is running you?

If your quick response is about success, paying the bills, graduating, making quota, finding the love of your life, pleasing your parents, or taking care of the family, you might want to dig a little deeper. Have you ever contemplated achieving those things without having to work so hard? Pushing hard for things can come from deep-seated beliefs about being inadequate, needing to work hard to feel valuable, and needing to work hard for money, to name a few.

For example, if somewhere in your psyche is an imprint picked up long ago that you're not enough, you will run yourself ragged trying to be enough. Maybe you feel like you need multiple degrees or certifications so others will "see" you and what you have to offer. Or perhaps you work incessantly to please your parents or spouse, never giving yourself a break, and still never feeling like you're doing enough. Perhaps you don't feel like you can say no to peers or colleagues who want you to do things their way, because you're afraid they will withhold their love, respect and support. Or maybe you simply settle for what shows up rather than making it clear what you really want and waiting for that.

If you can relate to any of these, ask yourself if it's time to stop the madness! Connect with your deepest beliefs about the things you are pushing for or struggling to create. Are those beliefs serving you or are they running you ragged? Are you feeling uplifted and peaceful as you write and review the list, or are you feeling sad, angry, frustrated or lost? If it's more of the latter, those emotions are telling you something about your inner state. Are you ready to listen?

Remember the **Shake Up!** Step. Don't just settle for the stories you're telling yourself about why you're chasing after whatever it is you're chasing, or settling for whatever you're settling for. What could be under the surface that is the real source of your apparent "need" or desire to be a certain way, have a certain something, or accomplish a certain goal? The more you get clear on the hidden drivers beneath all of your conditioned patterns of response, the greater are your opportunities to change those drivers. When you do that, your response patterns will change as well.

Also know that when you find yourself pushing and struggling, it might be because you are out of alignment with whatever it is you are seeking. You can't manifest your highest potential if you're vibrating at a level that's way beneath that. You'll need to know what inside you is creating alignment with the vibrations of working hard, struggle, or pushing, and then release it to align with higher vibration experiences like ease, synchronicity, and serendipity.

Then once you head down the path toward greater alignment with your highest Consciousness by releasing the emotional-junk-in-your-trunk that is subconsciously running you ragged, you can more peacefully and patiently trust and receive as your highest good unfolds. I know how difficult it can be to rest in trust, and allow good to come. This can be especially tough if you are healing conditioned patterns of behavior and thought that are about working hard, being productive, and taking care of everything.

You might wait patiently at first, but then feel yourself getting anxious, wondering if anything is really happening. You may see lack of movement or opportunity as a sign that nothing has changed. You may judge the quiet and peace you feel as a problem instead of a Blessing. You may be asking yourself if you've done enough, prayed enough, believed enough, healed enough.

In fact, you probably have done plenty. Perhaps what you haven't done enough of is release attachment to the timing of the outcome. You may

> **P**erhaps what you haven't done enough of is release attachment to the timing of the outcome.

still be trying to control how and when everything works out. You may be impatiently demanding that everything happens according to your ideas and timing.

This attachment to how everything unfolds can disturb and lower the vibration you just raised. Impatience with the unfoldment can cause doubt, and doubt tends to bring up fear, and fear is about the lowest emotional vibration there is. You can't manifest your highest good when you're vibrating at the level of fear. So do your best to remain positive in the in-between places.

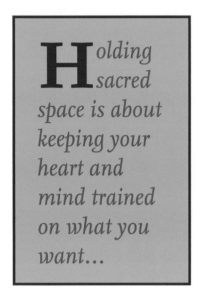

Holding sacred space is about keeping your heart and mind trained on what you want...

In-between places are like a void—a place where you know the old ways in which you operated will no longer work, and the new you is still taking shape. You'll find this is an ongoing dance as you apply the **4 Steps** over time. Don't worry, you will get accustomed to it, and soon you'll find yourself recognizing when you're in an in-between place. Instead of worrying that nothing is happening, you'll be grateful for an opportunity to hold sacred space for what is coming next.

Holding sacred space is about keeping your heart and mind trained on what you want, what you are creating, and how you want to feel. It's about recommitting to you. It's about holding yourself to the highest standards of detachment and self-care, such that you are a perfect vessel to receive what is on its way. Keep applying the **4 Steps**, and keep expecting the good stuff to come in. It will.

One morning after meditation early in my own transformational journey, I was wondering why everything was taking so long. I felt like I had done some deep emotional release, and felt very much like old ways of being and expressing were dying or dead. But I still couldn't see the fruits of my labor. Money wasn't magically appearing, the love of my life hadn't asked me to dance, and major aspects of my life still felt difficult and disappointing. What worked the best for me was noticing what was coming up (mostly fear that I wasn't working hard enough to make things happen) and then applying the **4 Steps** over and over, sometimes many times in a single day. That's how I confirmed they worked. I also doubled-down on my gratitude practice, ensuring that I was finding even the tiniest of things for which to be grateful that I could celebrate as a way of validating myself and how well I was doing on my own behalf.

Whatever negative conditioned patterns you are reprogramming, they were not created in a blink of an eye. They are the result of habitually thinking, believing and acting on ideas that are out of alignment with your Divine Self. Embrace the time it may take to shift yourself into a new inner place.

I found this poem and share it here to help you rest in faith and trust as things unfold for you on Divine timing. It was written by Pierre Teilhard de Chardin (1881–1955), French philosopher and Jesuit priest:

> Above all, trust in the slow work of God.
> We are quite naturally impatient in everything
> to reach the end without delay.
> We should like to skip the intermediate stages.
> We are impatient of being on the way to something
> unknown, something new.
> And yet it is the law of all progress
> that it is made by passing through
> some stages of instability –
> and that it may take a very long time.
>
> And so I think it is with you,
> your ideas mature gradually—let them grow,
> let them shape themselves, without undue haste.
> Don't try to force them on,
> as though you could be today what time
> (that is to say, grace and circumstances
> acting on your own good will)
> will make of you tomorrow.
>
> Only God could say what this new spirit
> gradually forming within you will be.
> Give God the benefit of believing
> that his hand is leading you,
> and accept the anxiety of feeling yourself
> in suspense and incomplete.

Change Your Routines

Choose your most prominent and frequent routines and mix it up a little—or a lot. Do something totally different from what you normally do. The idea is to be as flexible and free of attachments as possible. As you consciously choose to change it up, you'll engage different muscles—from your brain to your fingers and toes—and you'll see and experience things differently. You could meet new people, discover new desires, and mark a new path. A whole new world could open up from a minor shift in how you do what you typically do.

- ♥ If you walk, ride a bike; if you ride a bike, go for a swim.

- ♥ If you meditate inside, go outside. If you don't meditate at all, do it at least 2 min a day, then bump up to five minutes a day as soon as possible, and try to get up to at least 30 minutes a day.

- ♥ Turn the radio off in your car and listen to an uplifting or educational CD instead. If you already do the educational CD thing, listen to classical music instead.

- ♥ Take a day off from church and experience the Divine through selfless service in your community.

- ♥ Give the gardener or the sprinkler system a day off and hand-water your garden. Talk to the plants lovingly while you do, and feel the peace and love that radiates inside you. Choose to integrate this as a once-a-week practice.

- ♥ Brush your teeth with the opposite hand for a week. After that, continue to switch back and forth between both hands until it feels comfortable brushing from both.

- ♥ Find a trail or path to hike or jog on that you've never been on before.

- ♥ Find a new route to wherever you generally drive.

- ♥ Radically change your eating habits for a day or more. Give up animal protein and sugar. Eat live food and experience the difference it makes in how you think and feel.

💜 If you already do yoga, try a different studio or style or new way to challenge yourself.

💜 If you regularly do anything on a certain schedule, change the activity and/ or change the schedule.

💜 Try-on someone else's routines. How do they fit? How do you feel differently about their life and perspective as a result?

💜 Anytime you hear yourself wanting to say "I've always done it this way," consciously choose to change the way you do whatever it is.

List some of your own ideas.
What routines are you ready to change?

_____

_____

_____

_____

_____

_____

_____

_____

_____

_____

_____

_____

_____

_____

_____

_____

_____

_____

_____

_____

_____

_____

_____

Practice Capturing Yourself

What feelings are you experiencing as you work with the Steps?

If you want to manifest the new...
Bless and release the old you.

_____
_____
_____
_____
_____
_____
_____
_____
_____
_____
_____
_____
_____
_____
_____
_____
_____
_____
_____

Engage Your Five Senses

We can often take the world for granted because we rely on our senses for our experiences. Because we don't have to *think* about seeing, smelling, hearing, touching, or tasting, we tend to engage on autopilot all the time. Imagine what it would be like to deliberately engage your senses in order to change your experience. Notice what you notice through the other senses when one sense is disengaged. Also notice how you feel as you focus on using a sense that you don't engage in as often, like touching. Are you pressing up against the artificial boundaries your Rules of Engagement created for you? Are those boundaries serving you?

- ♥ Eat your favorite meal blindfolded. (There are actually restaurants that offer "dining in the dark!") Can you notice differences in the tastes relative to when you can see what you're eating?

- ♥ Spend a day in silence—don't speak to anyone. How do you feel without the ability to engage using your voice and ability to articulate?

- ♥ Block outer sounds using earplugs or another means. Then observe a conversation between two people, sit in nature, wander a busy street. How does your experience of these situations change when you can only *see* your environment without your ability to hear?

- ♥ Go through an entire day blindfolded and *hear* your experiences without seeing them. Listen to music, take a bubble bath, sit in a garden, explore the mall, walk the beach, have a conversation. No peeking!

- ♥ If you wear glasses and can safely spend a day without them, try it. How does it feel to see differently? What do you notice about how you routinely engage the world with your glasses versus without them?

♥ Eat a type of food or cuisine you've never experienced. You could try adding different types of fresh herbs, an unusual fruit or vegetable, or cheese to your salad or other dish. You could explore unfamiliar foods at restaurants with Ethiopian, Vietnamese, German, or Persian cuisine—whatever is unusual for you—and make it an adventure. See if you can find at least 25 different items that you've never tasted before. What do you learn about the Ethiopian, Vietnamese, German and Persian people through their food? How does consciously choosing to grow your palette change your view of the cultures related to each cuisine?

♥ Walk in the woods and make note of the colors, sounds, and smells you experience along the way. See how the sun comes through the treetops, or the leaves crunch under your feet. Touch different plants and note the difference in the feel of the leaves, flowers, and branches.

♥ Spend a day touching people as you speak with them. Go beyond the handshake greeting. What feelings does incidental touch bring up as you touch others? What feelings does it bring up when you are touched by others? Do you feel more empathy? Do you feel violated? Explore your touch boundaries and what beliefs and stories they are coming from.

♥ Explore your relationship with your physical body. What do you feel when you see yourself in the mirror? What do you hear when you notice yourself walking? What does your touch feel like to you? Can you tell when you are fully connected with yourself through the sensate nature of the physical body?

Draw a picture or add photographs of your sensory adventures.

Capture your own experiences of your five senses here.

To discover the joy in the treasure within you must first go on the hunt.

Reconnect Deeply with Nature

Our ancient ancestors knew something we've all but forgotten: We have a Divine connection with nature and all sentient beings. When we nurture that connection, we not only receive Divine guidance and wisdom, we also feel more peace, joy, and freedom. Go to a natural place as far from civilization as possible and spend an entire day communing with nature.

- ♥ Listen to the sounds and see if you can identify the creatures. Take a journal and write about your feelings as you share time with Mother Earth and her bounty.

- ♥ Take a sketch pad and pencils and draw what you see, or use paint and instead of brushes, use only the elements you find in nature as your instruments of creation.

- ♥ Lie on your back and look up at the trees. What do you see and how does it make you feel? What images do you see in the clouds?

- ♥ Soak up the morning dew with your feet. Walk barefoot outside, feeling the grass, dirt or sand between your toes. What memories come up?

- ♥ Take a walk on a safe trail with your eyes closed. Listen to the sounds and connect with your feelings. Can you hear what nature is saying to you? How are you trusting as you walk without seeing?

- ♥ Try things that help you feel the awesomeness of nature. Swim in the ocean or a big lake. Lie in a field at night and explore the sky, taking in the stars and moon. Walk in the woods or on the beach during a full moon. See what images you see in clouds.

- ♥ Climb a tree and look out over the area surrounding it. How do you feel getting a more bird's-eye view? What do you notice about the surroundings that you hadn't noticed from a previous vantage point?

♥ Find a way to personally care for nature in some way in your area. How do you feel connecting with the plants/animals you serve? Do you feel connected or separate?

♥ Have an animal card reading and see what animals might be your spiritual totems or guides. Have you noticed them in your life before? How well do you relate their meaning with your life's situations? Can you feel how to incorporate their gifts to help you with your conscious choices as your life continues to unfold?

♥ Sleep under the stars. How does it feel to be in a natural setting instead of your bed? What do you notice about your relationship with and feelings in nature after darkness falls versus in the daylight?

If you want peace and purity,

Doodle Page

tear away your coverings. ~ Rumi

Doodle Page

Everything you gain in life will rot or fall apart. All you have left is what is in your heart. ~ Jim Carrey

Disconnect From All Technology for an Entire Day (or more)

Are your constantly plugged into your computer, smart phone, gaming device, or some other form of technology? It may seem like no big deal, but there is a cost. A University of London study found that constant electronic connection, like emailing and texting, actually reduced mental capacity by an average of ten IQ points! But that's not all.

You see, when your brain is forced to be "on alert" all the time, you're living in what's called a "fight or flight" state. This causes wear and tear on your central nervous system, which, over time, will considerably shorten your life. YUCK.

But here's the kicker. Even with all of these ways to supposedly get and stay connected through technology, the opposite is happening. We're actually more disconnected from each other, and ourselves than ever before. With your happiness and peace at stake, it is time to pay particular attention to your relationship with technology, and how it might not be serving you. It's probably time to do something to get OFF the technology-induced "on alert" status by trading device time for time spent engaging through the activities below.

- ♥ Spend an entire day without your phone, computer, or any other form of technological support (Don't even carry the technology with you where you go). Note how you feel. When do you feel anxious and what's causing the anxiety? How long does it take for you to feel peaceful and safe?

- ♥ Build no-technology time into each day. Start with 30-minutes, and build up to what feels good. I start the first two hours of my day without checking my phone or computer so I can devote my attention to myself.

- ♥ Visit people instead of texting, emailing, or calling them.

- ♥ Handwrite a letter to someone you've been meaning to reconnect with, and mail it via snail mail.

♥ Commit to regularly writing thank-you notes for gifts and kindnesses you receive.

♥ Have a family dinner where everyone helps shop for and prepare it. Instead of watching TV, connect and share conversation about what's going on in the family.

♥ Have a family game night and play some oldies-but-goodies like Charades, Rummy 500, or Monopoly. Or have a family craft night and engage in your individual and collective creativity.

♥ Get some friends together that you've been meaning to introduce to each other. Play ice-breaker games to help people connect and get to know one another.

People to Visit:

_____
_____
_____
_____
_____
_____
_____
_____
_____
_____

Game Night—Who, What, Where, and When:

_____
_____
_____
_____
_____
_____
_____
_____
_____
_____
_____

Dinner Together:

_____

_____

_____

_____

_____

_____

_____

_____

_____

_____

_____

_____

_____

_____

_____

_____

_____

_____

My Unplugged Days:

Doodle Page

Helpguide.org lists numerous physical, mental, and social benefits from humor and laughter. Among them are boosting the immune system, relieving tension in the body, releasing endorphins, helping protect the heart, relieving stress, shifting perspective, enhancing team relationships, and promoting group bonding.

My favorite laughter practice is laughter yoga because it doesn't require me to engage my intellect in order to laugh. It's laughter for no reason. People start

laughing, even if it's somewhat forced, and then they allow the laughter to expand and deepen to access true inner joy. Whatever way you can, make getting your laugh on a conscious practice as part of your **Happy to Be ME!** Lightstyle. Give yourself the gift of laughter for 20-minutes or more, as often as you can.

♥ Go see a comedy movie or play.

♥ Find a laughter yoga practice in your area and sign-up for classes.

♥ Find a joke book or website and enjoy the jokes several times a week.

♥ Find good stand-up and/or improv comedy and go at least once-a-month.

♥ Be sure to have a healthy laugh at yourself when it's warranted.

♥ Invite some friends over and have a laugh-a-thon. See who can laugh longest and hardest. Who can do more kinds of laughter—giggly laughter, spooky laughter, outrageous laughter; SILENT laughter is really funny.

Doodle Page

Taking time to do nothing often brings everything into perspective. ~ Doe Zantamata

Doodle Page

Give Yourself a Break Day

Take a day to indulge yourself in ways that make you feel good, or give you a new/ better perspective. Ideally, this would be a day when you typically "work." The idea is to begin to integrate work and play more by morphing from one to the other *during* the week. This breaks up the typical routine of sliding from the workweek into the weekend on Saturday, and back out on Monday.

For many people, the idea of self-indulgence is difficult to embrace. If this is you, gently resist the urge to judge yourself. Suspend your disbelief and anxiety, and go for it. It is important that this does *not* become a day of catching up on chores or things you "have" to do. Allow yourself to be treated to something pleasurable, instead of always having to do it for yourself. Free yourself from constantly being in the position of giver, or from receiving from others, and allow yourself to receive from yourself. Commit to making this day about nurturing your body, feeding your Spirit, or soothing your Soul.

- ♥ Darken your room and sleep in as long as you can. Forget the workout, or anything else that takes you away from really indulging in you. When you think you've been in bed way too long, stay there some more. Just *be*... in your bed with you, your breath, and your presence. Allow yourself to doze. Relax.

- ♥ Read something uplifting. No politics or reality, no murder mysteries or romance novels. Choose something that raises your vibration on the Consciousness scale. The poetry of Rumi or Hafiz, the wisdom of spiritual masters like Sri Satya Sai Baba or Shakti Gawain, the peaceful prose of Maya Angelou or Marianne Williamson. Choose one of your favorites and be with it fully.

- ♥ Go for a peaceful drive in an unfamiliar area or neighborhood. Then check out the local hotspots.

- ♥ Go to a park, lie on a blanket and look up at the sky. Feel the expanse of the space. Take a nap or meditate, or both.

♥ Get a 30-60 minute foot massage or 60-90 minute full-body massage. If you're on a budget, go to a local massage school and have a student serve you. It will be less expensive than going to a spa, but probably just as good.

♥ Even if you don't really need to, go to the salon and allow someone else to shampoo your hair and massage your scalp.

♥ Get a manicure. Many manicure places are inexpensive and offer free shoulder massage with your manicure! Guys, you'll feel rested and indulged this way too!

Capture your favorite indulgent ideas here...
then go experience them.

_____
_____
_____
_____
_____
_____
_____
_____
_____
_____
_____
_____
_____
_____
_____
_____
_____
_____
_____
_____
_____
_____
_____

I am going to be the love I came here to be...

_____
_____
_____
_____
_____
_____
_____
_____
_____
_____
_____
_____
_____
_____
_____
_____
_____
_____
_____
_____
_____
_____
_____

... starting first and foremost by giving some to me!

Doodle Page

YOU in YOUR WORLD

Connecting with the World That Reflects You

FOR MORE HAPPINESS, EAT PEAS AND GRAPES!

I can sometimes be overheard murmuring my favorite mantra. Once when this happened, the friend who heard me asked, "Did you just say eat peas and grapes?" It was a funny misinterpretation and I laughed as I thought about it for a moment. I do love eating that's for sure. It's probably one of my all-time favorite things to do. The exquisite tastes and textures, the friends I share it with – make eating a heartwarming ritual.

I don't like peas though. They are my 'Green Eggs and Ham'. As a pre-teen, I didn't get excused from the dinner table unless I belonged to the "clean plate club." When peas were on the menu, I would sit there looking at my almost-clean plate, with its pile of peas sitting there all cold and forlorn.

> **E**ase is holding the posture of a "YES!" in your body, mind, heart and Spirit...

But that was until I figured a way out. I'd put them in my mouth, quietly spit them into my napkin, and discreetly and oh-so-secretly empty the napkin into the waiting mouth of my dog Taffy who was patiently waiting under the table. She saved me from hours of sitting and staring at food I couldn't eat. Thanks girl.

However, childhood stories aside, neither peas nor grapes can transform your life. What my dear friend misheard is my mantra, "Ease, Peace and Grace." Now that's a phrase to embody!

When I simply utter the word ease, I feel an exhale. Ease is about releasing resistance within. Ease is holding the posture of a "YES!" in your body, mind, heart and Spirit, and using that energy for whatever shows up. Ease means allowing.

Ease within you is what you want as you respond to the difficult experiences of the day. Ease can be the gift that you give yourself in the midst of what appear to be the '**not** gifts' coming to you. It's the basis of your ability to embrace a day full of challenges and disappointments, struggles and conflicts, without loosing your cool and composure.

I love taking long beach walks. Where I walk, there is a combination of sand and rocks of different sizes, and sometimes, the tide creates hilly areas along the coast. Each walk is a surprise; the beach might be flat, smooth and rock-free, or the exact opposite. I can never know or predict what I will get and that's ok. Ease is about greeting whichever scenario I encounter with an open heart. The energetic "YES!" means I am open to whatever shows up—whether it's a flat, smooth and clean path, or whether I must step over rocks, pick up garbage, or pray over a dead pelican or gull. However, in our lives, it's often the unknown we resist the most. Consider this quote from Eckhart Tolle:

> ## Being at ease with not knowing is crucial for answers to come to you.

This is the beauty of your heart at ease—being an energetic "YES!" lets you receive more possibilities because you are not disrupting life's flow with the energy of resistance. Start to consciously notice how and when you are not allowing ease to be a part of who you are.

Ease is a starting point that can lead you to a deeper place. Ease is the surface layer of your inner state of Peace, which is a space of trust and openness, where there is the unmistakable knowing that everything is exquisitely right, regardless of appearances. Peace is your Essence—it's your State of Being.

I mentioned praying over a dead pelican or gull earlier as a potential beach walk experience. Ease is accepting that your walk includes a dead pelican, and Peace is trusting that however it died, ultimately all is as it should be—even while your judging self might be looking for something or someone to blame for its death. Peace comes from choosing to transcend the situational aspects of a moment, while allowing those aspects to be exactly as they are. As Mahatma Gandhi taught:

> Each one has to find his peace from within. And peace to be real must be unaffected by outside circumstances.

Your Peace is always waiting for you in the I AMness of you. There is no opposite of that. Your fears, anxieties, angers, and sadnesses are not really the opposite of Peace. When they grip you tightly and you feel like you can't get free of them, they are showing that you have *disconnected* from your Peace. When a lamp gets unplugged, its light goes out. But the electricity that can fuel it is still there waiting for the lamp to be plugged back in. Inner Peace can absolutely be your experience in the midst of struggle, pain,  fear and sadness—the darkness of your life does not affect your access to your inner Light. As you practice transcending what is, even while you include it as perfect in the moment, you stay connected to the truest source of Peace within. It's how you trust that you have safety, security, stamina, guidance, endurance, and comfort even in the midst of a beach walk with hills, rocks, debris, dead creatures and huge unknowns along the way.

And finally, there is Grace, which is when we feel like something amazing happened that we're not sure we deserve. It's what mystically and Divinely plugs your lamp back in when you can't even reach the plug, and helps you traverse whatever is showing up on your path. Grace is experiencing the presence of God when we least expect to in our outer lives, because we are barely connected to that aspect of us within.

When you attach to the appearances of lack and limitation—being out of time and out of options—Grace is the gift of abundance and opportunity showing up anyway. Grace is what saves you when your vibration is attracting reflections of the false-self. It shows up to remind you of who and what you are, and that you can choose how to experience whatever is happening, right when you may be at your absolute worst place for remembering and choosing.

When you find yourself in the midst of situations that make you ask "Where did this come from?", Grace helps you take responsibility and love yourself anyway, without judgment, guilt, blame or shame. It keeps you whole when you realize that sometimes you're unable to claim the Divinity within you, and that you're attached to the limited ideas of your human self, experiencing fear, sadness and loneliness. As the poet Rumi says:

> ## Give up to grace. The ocean takes care of each wave till it gets to shore.

Grace is the Divine Love that you are, loving you.

Yes, I love to affirm Ease, Peace and Grace in my life always. I offer this mantra to you, and intend that it elevates your vibration so you can transcend the experiences of your life that are not at all easy, peaceful, or Grace-filled, and still claim your happiness.

Connect with Those Around You

I remember moving almost every 14-16 months as a young Marine Corps brat. And some school years, I went to two different schools in two different states. Every time we moved into a new neighborhood, generally on military bases, neighbors would welcome us, often by bringing casseroles and other goodies to make our first few days less burdensome. How many times have you been on the giving or receiving end of this sort of kindness and caring?

What about local businesses you frequent? Do you know the owners and regular staff? These days, it seems like people drive into their garages, close the door behind them and rarely engage people right next door. Between the growth of online shopping, gaming and socializing many people can go all day without real person-to-person interaction. A lot of people are feeling disconnected and isolated as a result. It's time to drop the barriers and connect with members of our communities! Give yourself an opportunity to share your love, light and wisdom with those around you, and allow yourself to receive the same from them.

- ♥ Be more neighborly. Knock on your neighbors' doors, say hello, share yourself, and get to know them. Keep a tablet in your kitchen with their names, so you can remember and call them by name when you say hello. Invite them over for dinner, to join you on a walk, or explore fun things in the neighborhood together.

- ♥ Develop your listening skills. For one whole day, resist the temptation to interject your perspective, suggestions, and stories into conversations with others, or into their realities. See if you have difficulty listening to someone with no personal agenda, with total acceptance.

- ♥ Visit the local school or community center weekly and do something selfless in the moment.

- ♥ Frequent the farmer's market and create relationships with the merchants you buy from the most. Have a conversation about how they're doing, not just the food you're purchasing. See how many similarities you share. Is there anything you can do to support them further? Can you see them as friend-worthy instead of just merchants?

♥ Suggest having a block party, ice cream social, barbecue, neighborhood clean-up or other ways to "commune" with your community. What can you learn about people that bridges you into a deeper connection with them?

♥ Host a "Come As You *Will* Be" party. Everyone comes as their future selves; they dress and talk as though they are living their dreams right now. Learn how you can support attendees to achieve their dreams and see how they can support you with yours.

Create a Happy Work Environment

The 2015 Conference Board Job Satisfaction survey, released in September, reports that "for the eighth straight year, less than half of US workers are satisfied with their jobs." I first read about this in the 2010 Survey, when the results were slightly worse, and had hit their lowest level in 22 years at 42.6%. While there may be many issues contributing to the low results, from my perspective, the centerpiece of the problem is that too many workers are stuck in the old model of deriving happiness from success. Data from the fields of positive psychology and neuroscience are turning the tables on the relationship between success and happiness, showing that success actually comes *from* happiness, rather than causing it.

Forbes Magazine and others report on America's Happiest Companies. Making the top 25 on the 2015 Forbes list are well-known and perhaps beloved brands like Johnson & Johnson (#1), Broadcom, Google, Chrysler, Microsoft, Intel and FedEx. Each of these is among a host of companies aiming to boost productivity by investing in their employees' general happiness. From clubs, positivity counseling, paid sabbaticals, paid meals/snacks, onsite childcare, game rooms, to lush campuses with organic gardens and health benefits for part-timers, creating a happy culture is a growing part of growth strategy globally.

Based on the number of firms that make the list at high numbers one year, only to drop completely from the top 50 the next year (Pfizer was #1 in 2014 and didn't make the list in 2015; Apple was #14 in 2014 and dropped to #50 on the 2015 list), it's not that easy to keep a happiness trend going, at least the way it's been tried by some companies on the list. I'm not surprised—until the strategies and tactics implemented by employers and embraced by employees address more the *inner* aspects of happiness, we're treating an internal festering wound with a lot of external topical salves.

Whether you are an employer looking to reap the happy employee rewards of lower turnover, greater productivity, lower healthcare costs, and a higher retention rate (to name a few), or an employee wanting to have a better time during the huge percent of your life that you spend at work, being happy at the office is critical to an integrated happier, more successful, more fulfilling life. Here are some ideas that can be just for you individually, and can also be implemented in work teams. The key to success is remembering that none of these individually or even collectively will take you as far into your deepest, truest and most *lasting* happiness as inner work using the **4 Steps**.

♥ Put some heart into the environment. Hold HeartMath classes to help people understand the power of integrating their hearts and heads, as Albert Einstein did. Help people speak from their gut reactions to situations, not just their analytical heads.

♥ Cultivate an optimistic culture. Actively look for ways to acknowledge, appreciate, and celebrate even the smallest of positive happenings, no matter the gravity of any situation.

♥ Resist making everything so serious. Create realistic timelines, let go of language that reinforces heaviness like "do or die," and be willing to classify some items on the things-to-do list as not very important at all.

♥ Keep people in the now. Meditation to quiet mind chatter, focusing on physical breathing, and engaging in sensory exercises are all ways to keep people more present.

♥ Make your staff feel heard, seen and regarded: 1) Actively and *objectively* listen when they're sharing ideas or concerns, 2) Acknowledge their efforts *regardless of impact*, and 3) Honor their uniqueness and allow them to be *authentic*.

♥ Create opportunities for staff to be the givers, receivers, or observers of acts of kindness and compassion within your organization. Allow staff to donate excess vacation or sick leave to colleagues who need it. Coordinate means for staff to contribute to the community through tree planting, neighborhood clean-ups, adopt-a-family, or collectively offering pro-bono services to the disadvantaged or non-profit organizations.

♥ Create opportunities for more onsite laughter. Start an improv comedy club and host shows during lunch, offer onsite laughter yoga classes, or encourage joke exchanges before meetings to get people laughing and feeling lighter and more present.

♥ Designate a "Happiness Zone"—physical space where only happiness can "happen." Encourage people to take time-outs once or twice a day (ensuring they see you leading the way). Fill the space with bright colors, music, joke books, playful activities that touch the inner child, and other engaging ways to recharge and release. Over time, there will be a "spillover effect," where the lighter, more peaceful, balanced feeling of the Zone begins to leak out and fill the entire office.

♥ Hire a Chief Happiness or Chief Culture Officer (I may be interested in that kind of corporate position!). Make it clear at all levels of your organization that happy, authentic, spiritually-awake people are valued. Give them responsibility for helping the staff raise their individual Consciousness to create a collective Consciousness that is more peaceful, happy, fun and abundantly successful.

Doodle Page

Doodle Page

I see my parents as tiny children who need love.
I have compassion for my parents' childhoods.
I now know that I chose them because they were
perfect for what I had to learn. I forgive them and
set them free, and I set myself free.

~ Louise Hay

Become a Selfless Server

As services diminish with budget cuts, many organizations and institutions that serve you and your family, and others in the community, are impacted. Schools are cutting arts and music classes; churches are cutting outreach to the under-privileged; community centers are reducing hours and programs, or closing altogether. Is there a way to give your time and talent to help your community thrive? You'll find that the real gift of giving is the joy you feel from helping others. And as you raise your Consciousness, the joy of giving will take on a whole new level of pleasure and fulfillment.

- ♥ Join Big Brothers/Big Sisters, a local Boys and Girls Club, or through another means, develop a meaningful relationship with a young person who needs a mentor.

- ♥ Volunteer at an elementary school. Read aloud, host a career experience that shows them what you do and how they can get onto that career track. Help with the annual talent show, or fix-up day.

- ♥ Everywhere you go for one day, smile the whole way. Smile at the people you see whether they smile back or not. Give big smiles to everyone. When they ask you how you are, tell them "Fabulous!" no matter what you're feeling. Be the selfless spreader of happy moments. How does it feel to actively engage strangers?

- ♥ Assist at a food bank or hospital and feel gratitude for your abundance and good health.

- ♥ Beautify the environment. Join or create a committee at your church or school to help keep the grounds looking nice. Hold clean-up days in local parks and adjacent areas. Keep trash bags in your car, and wherever you go, pick up litter and dispose of it properly.

- ♥ Help lead a youth ministry or provide daycare to children at your church.

♥ Join a Habitat For Humanity group in your area and help get people off the streets.

♥ Walk dogs or help give love to sick and boarded pets at the local veterinarian. Take treats to or provide foster care to animals at the local animal shelter.

♥ Volunteer with your City Council, School Board, Energy Commission or other public organization working for the health and vitality of your community.

♥ Go on a mission trip to a foreign country. Pack an extra suitcase of your gently used clothing and new toiletries, and donate them to people in need.

♥ Become a hugger to sick children or premature newborns in the hospital. Center your heart on love and healing as you share the powerful energy with the kids.

♥ Everywhere you go for one day, pay people compliments, whether you know them or not. Be sincere in finding at least one thing you can appreciate about them. How does it feel to consciously look for something to appreciate in everyone?

For many of us, our knowledge and understanding of our neighborhoods starts and stops with the routes we frequent. We rarely, if ever, take time to get off the beaten path and get to know our surroundings intimately. Even if we do, we may take things for granted. Our lives can be enhanced by recognizing the gifts that are around us all the time.

What might you be missing that could be a part of your unfolding alignment with your Higher Consciousness? What's hiding in plain sight right around you that is waiting to be included in your life? I remember finishing one of my favorite spiritual books, and noticing on the back inside cover that the author's biography mentioned that she lived in a "Southern California beach community." I said to myself "Hey! I live in a Southern California beach community!" I connected with her, and through her organization, a whole group of like-hearted spiritual women and men to continue my awakening and unfolding, and with whom to share playful activities.

A similar Divine connection may be awaiting you at this very moment. Get out there and explore what is off your beaten path, and see what happens.

- ♥ Take a camera and photograph the obscure and different aspects of your community. Really get to know and appreciate them, from the buildings to the bugs. What tickles your fancy?

- ♥ Visit a local farm or farmer's market and buy fresh produce, eggs or meat directly from the farmer. You can find organic farmers at http://www.localharvest.org/ and farmer's markets at http://www.ams.usda.gov/local-food-directories/farmersmarkets. How does it feel to shop directly from the grower rather than through big grocery corporations? How does the food taste?

- ♥ Put out some bird seed, or a hummingbird feeder, and see what different kinds of birds come to visit you. What is there to learn about the species that is important for you? What do they represent spiritually? Take some time to appreciate and admire them, and feel what happens inside you as you do.

- ♥ Explore the unseen territory that surrounds your life. What parks or playgrounds have you never visited? What libraries or bookstores have you never visited? What little ethnic bodegas or quirky gift shops have you shunned? Explore them now, being very conscious of what stirs inside you calling for an even deeper exploration.

- ♥ Visit locally-owned restaurants, shops, and cafés. Get to know the owners and regulars. Create a community within the community.

- ♥ See if there is a local gem/mineral/geology club and go rock-hounding with them.

- ♥ Find out about the history of the land where you are. How can you honor its past as you continue toward the future?

- ♥ Does the local art gallery sponsor shows in support of local artisans? Who attends? What might you have in common with them?

- ♥ Look up the national monuments and parks in your area. Many of them are never visited. Find one that's new to you and go experience it up close and personal.

- ♥ Share some love with the natural environment. Literally hug a tree. Stop to admire a flower and tell it how beautiful you think it is. Share a little of your personal energy with EVERY natural thing you see as you walk, admiring how unique and special it is, how intelligent it is to grow from a small seed into something so complex and beautiful. See how deeply you can feel your connection to all that is.

Doodle Page

Doodle Page

Wrapping it Up

CULTIVATE AN ATTITUDE OF GRATITUDE
How Thankfulness Makes a Difference

Let not your mind run on what you lack as much as on what you have already. ~ Marcus Aurelius

I have mentioned gratitude throughout the book. It is one of the highest vibrations you can create within yourself, boosting your attractive force to bring you more for which to be grateful. As Marcus Aurelius reminds you, everything you have already is worthy of your gratitude.

When people are faced with significant challenges they can find it hard to be grateful. Perhaps this is you? If you're feeling like you're already struggling to find happiness, fulfillment and success, you may believe you have to wait for that stuff to show up before you'll have much for which to be grateful. I encourage you to rethink that now.

No matter what is going on that has you feeling like your life is full of problems and disappointments, you don't need to send your vibration into the darkness. Stop telling the story of the tough situation; stop ruminating about the situation; stop worrying over the situation. Don't let yourself get stuck in the negative. Personal

development guru, Chuck Gallozzi, calls this condition "negativitis" and says it's almost as pervasive as the common cold, but far more serious. You see, it's impossible to be happy when you're complaining. It's also difficult to find solutions, and you may even be making yourself sick, literally. When focused on the problem, your brain is engaging in the dynamics of the problem, and it's harder for the low-hanging-fruit solutions to become apparent. Your negativity creates stress related to the situation, which, in turn, can cause heart disease, ulcers, and weaken your immune system, making you susceptible to other health problems. Yes, your thoughts affect your immune system, and people like Chuck, who study psychoneuroimmunology, can help you see the damage you're doing. As Chuck points out:

> Everything negative we say *about* ourselves *to* ourselves and to others is a suggestion. We are unwittingly practicing self-hypnosis, programming ourselves for failure and creating self-fulfilling prophecies.

One way to get out of everything, from the not-so-great to the doom-and-gloom scenarios of your life is to consciously practice an attitude of gratitude. According to Dictionary.com the term "gratitude" is derived from the Medieval Latin word *gratitude* and Latin *gratia*, which are associated with the terms "grace," "gratefulness," and "graciousness." To me, these suggested the ideas of kindness and generosity, and the beauty of receiving. Gratitude is a centerpiece of the major religious and spiritual practices the world over. It has also been the focus of several studies into its correlation with health and well-being.

These studies have shown that gratitude not only increases happiness, life satisfaction, purpose, and self-acceptance, it also lowers stress and depression.

Grateful people show less problem avoidance, blame, and denial, and they're less likely to succumb to substance abuse as an escape.

Below are three practices from the studies that were proven to produce the most significant positive effects among the study participants. Importantly, the people in the studies still had things going on in their lives that were stressful, disappointing, and debilitating. Yet practicing gratitude in the midst of these things, made a real emotional, psychological, and physiological difference. Immerse yourself in gratitude right here and now and begin to heal your life. Choose one or try all three.

1. Do gratitude meditations daily. Hold grateful thoughts for a person or situation in your mind and heart for a minimum of five minutes. Do this at least once daily.

2. Pay a gratitude visit on someone special in your life. Write and personally deliver a letter of gratitude to a person you want to thank for how they've contributed to your life.

3. Keep a gratitude journal. On a daily basis, write down three to four things for which you are grateful. Commit to keeping the journal for a minimum of one month. If you're like the study participants, your results will be so positive that you'll keep this going for many months to come.

Gratitude Quotes and Poems

Here are a couple of my favorite thoughts on gratitude to help you get started shifting to an attitude of gratitude right here, right now.

> You simply will not be the same person two months from now after consciously giving thanks each day for the abundance that exists in your life. And you will have set in motion an ancient spiritual law: the more you have and are grateful for, the more will be given you.
>
> ~ Sarah Ban Breathnach

Whatever our individual troubles and challenges
may be, it's important to pause every now and then to
appreciate all that we have, on every level. We need to
literally 'count our blessings,' give thanks for them, allow
ourselves to enjoy them, and relish the experience of
prosperity we already have.

~ Shakti Gawain

Blessed are those that can give without remembering
and receive without forgetting.

~ Author Unknown

Be Thankful

~ Author Unknown

Be thankful that you don't already have everything you desire,
If you did, what would there be to look forward to?

Be thankful when you don't know something
For it gives you the opportunity to learn.

Be thankful for the difficult times.
During those times you grow.

Be thankful for your limitations
Because they give you opportunities for improvement.

Be thankful for each new challenge
Because it will build your strength and character.

Be thankful for your mistakes
They will teach you valuable lessons.

Be thankful when you're tired and weary
Because it means you've made a difference.

It is easy to be thankful for the good things.
A life of rich fulfillment comes to those who are
also thankful for the setbacks.

GRATITUDE can turn a negative into a positive.
Find a way to be thankful for your troubles
and they can become your blessings.

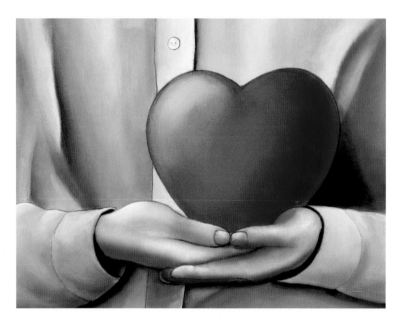

You can start *your* gratitude journal here...

_____

_____

_____

_____

_____

_____

_____

_____

_____

_____

_____

_____

_____

_____

CREATE YOUR PLAN
How Will You Embody The Principles?

And Now for Something Completely Different!
~ Monty Python's Flying Circus

This last activity is an opportunity for you to compile a guide to the themes and specifics that you have learned about yourself, and more importantly, how these learnings can be the foundation for new choices to take your life to a new level of alignment with your Highest Consciousness and its ideas of happiness for you. When you believe you are complete with the exploration for now (remember, you will want to reengage to keep yourself spiraling upward in your Consciousness), it's time to sum it all up and make some overall choices.

First, carve out some time to go back through and read whatever you captured along the way. You may want to use a highlighter to callout the most significant things you wrote. For example, highlight in yellow all the things that made you feel joyful and expansive. Then, highlight in pink all things that made you feel peaceful, calm and content; and highlight in green all the things that made you feel loved, and loving. Make sure you also highlight in another color that which brought up fear, sadness, anger or inner obstacles, and how you resolved them. Go through everything you've written to look for important or pervasive ideas.

Go to the next section called "My **Happy to Be ME!** Formula." Capture there the resolutions you are making that reflect the shifts in your relationship with yourself, your routines, and how you interact with the world. This journey of exploration and experiences should have brought you closer to knowing and living as the **Magnificent Essence** you already are. You may wish to share all or part of what you learned throughout the journey with the people closest to you, and ask them to support you in making choices that keep you on track. You may also encourage them to embark on their own journey to live **Happy to Be ME!**

If you are hearing more questions right now than answers, if you are feeling like your feelings are as clear as mud, if you are not sure of the best next thing to do, do not give up—do not even fret. Move into the place of neutral observer and trust that all is well. In the words of Bohemian-Austrian poet, novelist, and mystic, Rainer Maria Rilke:

> Be patient toward all that is unresolved in your heart and try to love the questions themselves.

The Themes from my Journey

My Personal **Living Happy to Be ME!** Formula

I'm excited that you've added yourself to the many who are putting these principles into embodied expression in their lives. Know that you are enhancing and expanding the ripple effect that is uplifting hearts and minds across the globe. Every time an individual endeavors to heal her past, raise his Consciousness, and step into a more self-aware, self-accepting, and self-loving expression, others are touched by their very presence. In fact, the energetic vibration resonates across the web of life to all beings regardless of the distance separating you. With that idea held in your heart and mind, it's a wonderful time to recite one of my favorite prayers...

METTA PRAYER*

May all beings be peaceful.

May all beings be happy.

May all beings be safe.

May all beings awaken to the light of their true nature.

May all beings be free.

*The Metta Prayer is an adaptation of the Karaniya Metta Sutta, a teaching on loving-kindness, from the Buddha.

And here's my invocation for how this book serves you:

May you make this way of living **your** Lightstyle,
and may your life be forever transformed as a result.

May your uplifted Consciousness contribute to a
planetary shift from fear to Love.

May you enjoy an overflowing cup of all that you desire.

May the best of your past be the worst of your future.

and

May you dance, laugh, play, and smile deeply inside at
the Magnificent Essence of you that is the heart and
Soul of your happiest life!

GOD BLESS!

BIBLIOGRAPHY

The following is a selected bibliography that offers insights into some of the ideas expressed in this book.

Abrams, Paula. "The Water Page - Water in Religion." The Water Page - Water in Religion. *Water Policy International Ltd*, 1 May 2003. Web. 20 June 2014. <http://www.africanwater.org/religion.htm>.

"Book Excerpt: Authentic Happiness." *ABC News*. ABC News Network, 02 Sept. 2010. Web. 15 Aug. 2011. <http://abcnews.go.com/GMA/story?id=125797>.

Achor, Shawn. *"The Happiness Advantage A New Method to Unlock Potential."* Common Ground. N.p., n.d. Web. 4 Sept. 2011. <https://www.stmatthewsday.org/ftpimages/472/download/Shawn%20Achor.pdf>.

Austin, Michael W. *"Achieving Happiness: Advice from Plato."* Achieving Happiness: Advice from Plato. Psychology Today, 11 Aug. 2010. Web. 2 June 2011. <http://www.psychologytoday.com/blog/ethics-everyone/201008/achieving-happiness-advice-plato>.

Cheng, Ben; Kan, Michelle; Levanon, Gad; and Ray, Rebecca L.: *Job Satisfaction: 2014 Edition*. Web. 24 May 2015. <https://www.conference-board.org/topics/publicationdetail.cfm?publicationid=2785>.

Childre, Doc Lew, Howard Martin, and Donna Beech. *The HeartMath Solution*. San Francisco, CA: HarperSanFrancisco, 1999. Print.

Ciotti, Gregory. *5 Scientific Ways to Build Habits That Stick*. n.d. Web. 10 July 2014. 99u.com <http://99u.com/articles/17123/5-scientific-ways-to-build-habits-that-stick>.

Chopra, Deepak. *The Ultimate Happiness Prescription: 7 Keys to Joy and Enlightenment*. New York: Harmony, 2009. Print.

Fontana, David. *Learn to Meditate: A Practical Guide to Self-discovery and Fulfillment*. San Francisco, CA: Chronicle, 1999. Print.

Gawain, Shakti, and Laurel King. *Living in the Light*. Mill Valley, CA: Whatever Pub., 1986. Print.

Goldthwait, John Ph.D. "Purifying the Heart." *The Convener*, Sri Sathya Sai Sadhana Trust, Publications Division, March 2010. Print.

Haslanger, Sally. "Plato on Happiness: The Republic's Answer to Thrasymachus." *Ancient Philosophy*. N.p., 25 Oct. 2004. Web. 2 June 2011. <http://ocw.mit.edu/courses/linguistics-and-philosophy/24-200-ancient-philosophy-fall-2004/lecture-notes/repsum.pdf>.

"Happy People Live Longer – Just Ask A Nun." Web log post. *The Hapacus Project*. N.p., n.d. Web. <http://www.thehapacusproject.com/2010/04/happy-people-live-longer-just-ask-nun.html>.

Hazelwood, JD. "Does The Mind's Chatter Ever Stop? | Buddhimudra - Awakening Body Mind Soul." *Does The Mind's Chatter Ever Stop? | Buddhimudra - Awakening Body Mind Soul*. N.p., n.d. Web. 15 Aug. 2011. <http://www.buddhimudra.com/wisdom/non-duality/75-does-the-minds-chatter-ever-stop>.

Hicks, Esther, Jerry Hicks, and Abraham. *Getting into the Vortex: Guided Meditations CD and User Guide*. Carlsbad, CA: Hay House, 2010. Print.

Hicks, Esther, and Jerry Hicks. *The Teachings of Abraham: How to Put the Law of Attraction to Work in Your Life*. London: Hay House, 2007. Print.

"Serotonin - The Molecule of Happiness." *HubPages*. N.p., n.d. Web. 2 Aug. 2011. <http://sriparna.hubpages.com/hub/Serotonin-The-Molecule-of-Happiness>.

Janis, Sharon. "Secrets of Spiritual Happiness." *SECRETS OF SPIRITUAL HAPPINESS: The Theories Behind Spiritual Happiness*. N.p., n.d. Web. 18 Aug. 2011. <http://www.spiritual-happiness.com/soshj.html>.

Lewis, Barbara and Jimmie. *Energy of Life*. Timonium, MD: Gemstone Publishing, 2002. Print.

Lamott, Anne. *Help Thanks Wow – The Three Essential Prayers*. New York, NY: The Penquin Group 2012. Print.

Luskin, Fred. "What Is Forgiveness?" Greater Good: The Science of a Meaningful Life. The Greater Good Science Center, University of California, Berkeley, 1 Jan. 2014. Web. 20 Aug. 2014. <http://greatergood.berkeley.edu/topic/forgiveness/definition#why_practice>.

McArthur, David, and Bruce McArthur. *The Intelligent Heart: Transform Your Life with the Laws of Love.* Virginia Beach, VA: A.R.E. / A.R.E./ Association for Research and Enlightenment, 1997. Print.

McErlane, Sharon. *A Call to Power: The Grandmothers Speak.* 2nd ed. N.p.: Net of Light, 2007. Print.

McGhee PhD, Paul. Humor: *The Lighter Path to Resilience and Health.* Bloomington, IN: AuthorHouse, 2010. Print.

"Meditation Techniques." *The Transcendental Meditation Program.* N.p., n.d. Web. 3 Nov. 2011. <http://www.tm.org/meditation-techniques?leadsource=CRM761>.

Miller, George A. "Theories of Learning in Educational Psychology." *George A. Miller, Information Processing.* N.p., n.d. Web. 2 Aug. 2011. <http://www.lifecircles-inc.com/Learningtheories/IP/GAMiller.html>.

Montenegro, Rosario. "How Dr. Hew Len healed a ward of mentally ill criminals with Ho'oponopono." Rosario Montenegro, N.P., n.d. Web. 27 Apr. 2014. Web. 27 Mar. 2011. <http://rosariomontenegro.hubpages.com/hub/How-Dr-Hew-Len-healed-a-ward-of-mentally-ill-criminals-with-Hooponopono>.

Myss, Caroline M. *Sacred Contracts: Awakening Your Divine Potential.* New York: Harmony, 2001. Print.

Paddison, Sara. *The Hidden Power of the Heart: Achieving Balance and Fulfillment in a Stressful World.* Boulder Creek, CA: Planetary Publications, 1992. Print.

Rosenbloom, Stephanie. "But Will It Make You Happy?" n.d.: n. pag. *The New York Times.* The New York Times, 08 Aug. 2010. Web. 16 Aug. 2010. <http://www.nytimes.com/2010/08/08/business/08consume.html?pagewanted=all>.

Ruiz, Miguel, Janet Mills, and Miguel Ruiz. *The Four Agreements Companion Book: Using the Four Agreements to Master the Dream of Your Life.* San Rafael, CA: Amber-Allen Pub., 2000. Print.

The Career Bliss Team: *CareerBliss 50 Happiest Companies in America for 2015. 8 Dec 2014. Web. 24 May 2015.* <http://www.careerbliss.com/facts-and-figures/careerbliss-50-happiest-companies-in-america-for-2015/>.

"The Power of Forgiveness" Journey Films. "Forgiveness and Justice" and "Forgiveness and Health." Web 27 Apr. 2014 N.p., <http://www. thepowerofforgiveness.com/index.html>.

Tolle, Eckhart. *The Power of Now: A Guide to Spiritual Enlightenment.* Vancouver, B.C.: Namaste Pub., 2004. Print.

University of Toronto, Rotman School of Management. "Time = Money = Less Happiness, Study Finds." *Medical Press.* 6 Feb. 2012. Web. 13 Mar. 2012. <http:// medicalxpress.com/news/2012-02-money-happiness.html>.

Veenhoven, Ruut. "How Do We Assess How Happy We Are? Tenets, Implications and Tenability of Three Theories." Address. New Directions in the Study of Happiness: United States and International Perspectives. United States, Notre Dame, IN. *University of Notre Dame.* Oct. 2006. Web. 11 June 2011. <http://www. nd.edu/~adutt/activities/documents/Veenhoven_paper.pdf>.

Water Policy International, Ltd. "Water in Religion." N.p., n.d. Web. 20 Jun. 2014 <http://www.africanwater.org/religion.htm>

Walkingfox, Sachen. "The Emperor Moth." Weblog post. *A Collection of Stories and Thoughts.* N.p., n.d. Web. 22 Sept. 2011. <http://www.sachem-uncas.com/ collection.html>.

Wauters, Ambika. *Chakras and Their Archetypes: Uniting Energy Awareness and Spiritual Growth.* Freedom, CA: Crossing, 1997. Print.

Whitworth, Eugene E. *Nine Faces of Christ: A Narrative of Nine Great Mystic Initiations of Joseph-Bar-Joseph in the Eternal Religion.* Marina Del Rey, CA: DEVORSS PUBLICATIONS, 1993. Print.

Wolf, Joshua Shenk "The Atlantic." *The Atlantic.* N.p., n.d. Web. 13 June 2011. <http:// www.theatlantic.com/magazine/archive/2009/06/what-makes-us-happy/7439/>.

Yogananda, Paramahansa. *Autobiography of a Yogi.* Los Angeles: Self-Realization Fellowship, 1971. Print.

Yogananda, Paramahansa. *The Yoga of Jesus.* Los Angeles: Self-Realization Fellowship, 2007. Print.

About the Author

Valerie Sheppard is a transformational teacher, speaker and author. She helps people experience more happiness, success and fulfillment. Using the **Living Happy to Be ME!** principles created from her own journey of spiritual transformation and shared in this book, her clients, from 15-80 years old, are healing past wounds, overcoming obstacles, and empowering themselves to create more vibrant lives and thriving businesses. She is a certified Sacred Contracts coach, and has been trained in compassionate communication, spiritual direction and HeartMath. She is also ordained through the Universal Life Church.

Valerie has a diverse coaching background spanning more than 25 years, including working with young people and adults through individual and group interactions. She is especially passionate about serving young adults, ages 17-25, with this message, and her big vision is to take the teachings of **Living Happy to Be ME!** global through her Happy and Whole Campus Initiative for colleges and universities. That work has begun through a pilot in partnership with the University of California, Irvine, where Valerie teaches life skills and personal leadership based on her book in a 10-week format called "Living 101: Being Happy and Whole."

Through her company The Heart of Living Vibrantly (http://HeartofLivingVibrantly. com), and its affiliated California-based 501c3 non-profit, Hearts Awakening (http://HeartsAwakening.org), Valerie provides individual and group coaching, workshops for organizations, schools, and corporations, and multi-day retreats. Valerie was awarded the 2015 *Unstoppable Award* from the Evolutionary Business Council, and was a 2012 nominee for the Orange County Business Journal's *Outstanding Women in Business Award* as well as the National Association of Female

Executives 2012 *Rising Star Award.* Her coaching principles are featured in the national best-seller *Everything is Subject to Change,* and she has been published in award-winning 11:11™ Magazine, Ezine, and is a Featured Luminary on InspireMeToday.com. She has been a guest on numerous national radio shows and covered by mainstream media, including MSNBC, Marketwire, and multiple ABC, NBC, and CBS television affiliates, to name a few.

Valerie lives in a Southern California beach community, where she does happy dances, drumming and searches for heart-shaped rocks on the beach, and is working on her second and third books. For more information, you can visit her website at http://HappytoBeME.net.

You can engage Valerie for:

Inspirational Speaking

In addition to her retreats and workshops, Valerie is a sought-after expert as a keynote, seminar or breakout speaker at conferences, meetings, seminars and other events. She has also emceed a number of events. In addition to her signature Happy to Be ME!© presentation, Valerie shares wisdom on these and other topics:

- Leadership Lessons from Improv Comedy
- 4 Ways Most Leaders Never Get "Great"
- Success is a Laughing Matter
- Engaging in Difficult Conversations

"Valerie Sheppard is a brilliant speaker who lights up the room with insight, intelligence and genuine guidance. She educates and elevates her audiences in success principles that motivate and inspire action." ~ Marsh Engle, Pasadena, CA

Spiritual Direction

Are you ready to claim your vibrant life? As your partner in transformation, Valerie can help you see yourself more clearly and support you to make changes to have more Peace, Love, Joy and Freedom! We offer a complimentary "From Tired to

Inspired" consultation. Connect and let us know what is going on with you and how you'd like it to be different.

"Valerie has helped me to examine important questions about myself. She keeps my focus on me even when I find I am looking towards outside sources for answers. She consistently identifies new ways of exploring issues that shed light on new and old problems. Her guidance has created balance, perspective, purpose and strategy. I feel more confident about my direction and Valerie has been an important part that." ~ Erin Moore, Vancouver, BC Canada

Consulting

Whether you want to enhance a corporate training program or institute a train-the-trainer laughter yoga initiative, Valerie's transformational training experiences create immediate impact and support long-lasting change.

"There is no way that Wicked Skatewear would be where it is today without the expertise, precision and guidance from Valerie Sheppard. As her intern during graduate school, soon friend and later a client, I am thankful each day of the opportunity to work with her. She provides more than just the day to day task oriented and report reading direction. There's a life awareness in and out of the workplace that is imperative for growth. Also - her smile and mood brightens ANY room!" ~ Bethany Semeiks, Partner, Wicked Skatewear

Contact Valerie

To inquire about engaging Valerie to speak at your next event, provide corporate training, or implement a Living 101 experience at your college or university, contact her at (949) 891-8491 or Info@HeartofLivingVibrantly.com.

To Learn More

Web:

http://HappytoBeME.net
http://HeartofLivingVibrantly.com
http://HeartsAwakening.org.

Twitter: @ValerieSheppard

LinkedIn: http://www.linkedin.com/in/valeriersheppard

Facebook: http://www.facebook.com/HeartofLivingVibrantly

Blog: http://heartoflivingvibrantly.com/blog

FREE Support: Join our FREE online community at www.HeartfulAwakenings. com and benefit from inspirational messages, periodic free monthly coaching calls and meditations, and Valerie's eBook, *Smooth Sailing: How to Move with Ease and Grace Through Every Situation.*

More praise for *Living Happy to Be ME!*

"I was thoroughly impressed with this guide book because of its practical nature. Happiness doesn't have to be hard but is required to live a fulfilled life! This is a must-have guidebook for anyone looking for the path to lasting Happiness. My dear friend Valerie Sheppard shows you how to take my favorite journey... from the head to the heart! This book has the potential to change millions of lives!" ~ DANIEL GUTIERREZ, AUTHOR, SPEAKER, TRANSFORMATIONAL LEADER AND RADIO PERSONALITY

"You will be compelled to go deeper and deeper into Valerie's book as soon as you begin reading. She provides a fresh perspective on how to become truly happy in your life." ~ JEANNIE S. WHYTE, FOUNDER OF WHYTE LIGHT CENTER, AUTHOR AND SPIRITUAL LIFE COACH

"What is happiness and how do we experience more of it? In this beautiful book, Valerie shares not only her own life lessons but also practical steps to help readers develop their own sense of happiness. You will want to keep coming back to it as you deepen your understanding of what it means to be truly happy." ~ PAT DUCKWORTH, AWARD-WINNING AUTHOR OF HOT WOMEN, COOL SOLUTIONS

"The book you are holding in your hands is the most remarkable, comprehensive self improvement book I have ever seen. Valerie speaks from deep experience, profound knowing and intuited wisdom. I love every word and give it my highest recommendation!" ~ MAUREEN ST. GERMAINE, PRACTICAL MYSTIC AND AUTHOR OF BEYOND THE FLOWER OF LIFE AND BE A GENIE

"Have you ever looked for happiness in the wrong places? Valerie Sheppard brings her fascinating perspective to the ages-old quest for happiness. She shares her precious lessons with us, giving us a process we can use to discover and become our unique happy selves. Want some more genuine soul-level happiness in your life? Get the book!" ~ PAUL HOYT, HOYT MANAGEMENT GROUP